STUDYING STRATEGIES

STRATEGIES 4

A CORE CONCEPT COURSE FOR THE FIRST CERTIFICATE EXAMINATION

Brian Abbs
Ingrid Freebairn
with
John Clegg
Norman Whitney

Contents

Word study techniques

This section is designed to help you to develop study techniques which you can apply throughout this book.

A reading exercise

Look at these words:

designer · develop · exhilarating · efficiently · gregarious · careless

If you met them in a text, would you

– ask your friend?
– ask your teacher?
– use a dictionary?
– guess?

Don't do any of these things yet. Read the passage below and then make a list of any words you do not fully understand.

'My name is Theresa Gomez. I come from Rio de Janeiro. I'm learning English because I need it for my work. In Brazil I'm a designer. I do a lot of artwork for magazines and it's important to be able to use English. I love Rio. It's exhilarating to live in a place where there's so much happening: good theatres, all the new films, concerts, discos! I'm a very gregarious person. I go out a lot and I like meeting people. I need to talk about the things that interest me, like art, social questions and world events. Sometimes though, I'm a bit careless. I need to develop better study habits because I don't read efficiently and I don't remember words easily. Sometime soon I want to take the Cambridge First Certificate examination and I need to practice for that too.'

The most efficient way of handling an unfamiliar word is to guess what it means by looking at the context.

Look at these examples:

'I'm learning English because I need it for my work. In Brazil I'm a [designer.] I do a lot of artwork for magazines and it's important to be able to use English.'

You know that [designer] is:

(a) a job

(b) a job which involves doing artwork for magazines.

Guess what it means. Write down a synonym (a word which means the same) either in English or in your language.

'I love Rio. It's [exhilarating] to live in a place where there's so much happening: good theatres, all the new films, concerts, discos!'

You know that [exhilarating] is:

(a) something positive

(b) something to do with living an active life: theatres, films etc.

Guess what it means. Write down a synonym either in English or your own language.

Sometimes you can guess what a word means by looking at its shape, like this:

careless: care- = attention; -less = without

Careless might mean 'without paying attention'.

Now look at all the words in your list and try to guess their meanings by looking at their context and their shape. Then compare your guesses with your partner.

A dictionary exercise

If you want to be *sure* you understand a word, use a dictionary.

Look at this extract from the LDOCE (Longman Dictionary of Contemporary English).
Compare it with the entry for designer **in your own dictionary.**

LDOCE	Information about the word	Can you find this in your dictionary? Put √ or ×.
de·sign·er /dɪˈzaɪnəʳ/ *n* a person who makes plans or patterns: *a designer of dresses/shoes/cars/an aircraft designer*	This is the *headword*. This is the *pronunciation*. This is the *grammatical information*. This is the *definition* These are *examples* of how to use the word.	....

Do you understand the information?

Look at another extract from the LDOCE.
Compare it with the entry for careless **in your own dictionary.**

care·less /ˈkeələs‖ˈkeər-/ *adj* **1** [B] not taking care; inattentive: *A careless driver is a danger to us all* **2** [A;(B)] not showing care or thought; done without care **3** [A] free from care; untroubled **4** [F (*about*); (B)] thoughtless; not worried: *He's careless about his family/about money matters* —**~ly** *adv* —**~ness** *n* [U]

LDOCE		Your dictionary
care·less	There may be more than one entry for the same word. Here there is only one.	How many entries are there for this word? Check that you have the right one.
/ˈkeələs‖ˈkeər-/	Different dictionaries have different systems for showing pronunciation. This one shows pronunciation and stress.	Can you pronounce the word? Look in the front and check that you understand the system the dictionary uses.
adj	This shows the word is an adjective.	Can you see what kind of a word it is? Look in the front and check that you understand the abbreviations the dictionary uses.
1	There may be more than one meaning for the headword. Here there are four.	How many definitions are there for the word in your dictionary?
[B]	This is more grammatical information. It shows where to use the word in a sentence.	Does your dictionary have this information? If so, check that you understand the abbreviations.
not taking care; inattentive:	This is the definition of the first meaning. It is also the meaning Theresa uses.	Which meaning in your dictionary is the one Theresa uses? Does it define the word in a similar way?
A careless driver is a danger to us all	This is a sentence showing how to use the word in its first meaning.	Does your dictionary have a similar example?
—**~ly** *adv* —**~ness** *n* [U]	Some entries show derivatives – related words with different endings. Here there are two, an adverb and an uncountable noun.	Does your dictionary show derivatives? Are they the same as these?

Now look up in your dictionary all the words on your list.
For each word:

- find its meaning
- pronounce it
- find out what its grammatical name is.

Remember: This is what to do when you come across an unfamiliar word:

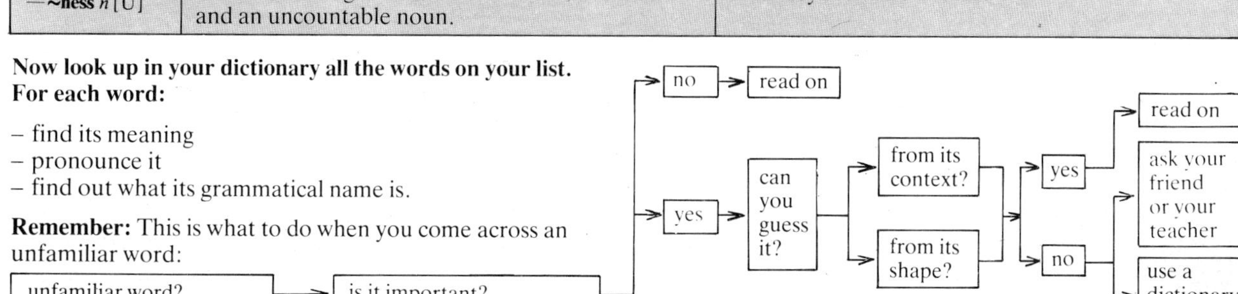

Unit 1 Take off!

Before you start:

What sort of holiday do you prefer?
Do you like staying in hotels or catering for yourself?
What sort of things do you buy when you go on holiday?
What can go wrong if you travel by car? by train? by boat? by plane?
What sort of presents do you like to take home?

'Well, with the children being quite young, we don't want to drive very far, but we do want to go abroad. It would have to be somewhere near the sea, though. The children love beaches. I've thought of France, actually, but Jack says it's very expensive.'

Mrs Crewe, Surbiton, Surrey

'My doctor says I need a complete rest and lots of fresh air. I was thinking of going to Switzerland – I do love the mountains – but I'm a bit frightened about going abroad alone. I don't speak any foreign languages.'

Nora Greene, Chester

'What are your plans for the summer, Mick?'
'I don't know yet. I've got six weeks so it's got to be cheap. I might get some sort of a job, I think.'
'You mean here in England?'
'No, never! I'm going to head for the sun.'

Mick Silver, student

'Julia, Martin and Jane have all got their holidays on the same dates so we could find something together. But not France. I went there last year. Somewhere hot where we can lie on the beach. Anyway, Jan, see what you can do.'

Lucy Adams, London

THE BELGIAN COAST offers you safe, sandy beaches – lively night-life – fascinating excursions – all just a hop across the Channel. Ask for a copy of our latest brochure featuring value-for-money holidays by air, sea or with your own car.
Cass Holidays Ltd.,
146 High Street, Epping,
Essex.
Tel: Epping 76888

EASY-GOING COMPANION wanted for travel to Italy and further, end of July until October; possibly working? 020-552971.

GRAPE-PICKING in the SOUTH OF FRANCE Depart by coach, Victoria Coach Station, September 15, 22 travel only. £28. Tel: 937 1908.

NAIROBI, overland via Sahara, Zaire gameparks, October 7th. £550. 340-7598.

GREECE Corfu, Crete, Paxos. The Greek Island villa specialists for nearly 9 years. We feature in our brochure some of the best villas currently available in Greece – houses with private beach or pool (self-catering or fully staffed); village houses; studios for 2 our speciality. Prices include maid. Flight from £150/£250 per person 2 weeks.
Tel: 01-700 0855/6.

NORWAY offers so many things you look for in a perfect holiday: the superb food, the uncrowded roads, the midnight sun – and the daylight sun . . . much more than many people think. The ever-changing landscapes of forests, mountains, beaches, flowered meadows and those spectacular fjords. Everywhere, when you do meet people, they're so friendly – and most speak English.

1

Match the people with the right holiday above and say why you think the holiday would be suitable, like this:

I think the Crewe family would most enjoy a holiday . . .

because [it / they / there] is/isn't . . . would/wouldn't . . .

2 

EAST-WEST DISCOVERY
14 nights from £494 inc. air fares and accommodation. The best of two coasts. (Departures weekly on Fridays).

Pat and Mike have always wanted to go to America. This summer they have saved up enough money to go on a two-week trip to the East and the West coasts – Mike tells a friend about it.

MIKE: Well, we're off next Friday!
SUE: Where to?
MIKE: The States.
SUE: Really! How wonderful! I've never been there myself. How long are you going for?
MIKE: Two weeks.
SUE: Why did you choose America? Have you got friends there?
MIKE: No, we've always wanted to go. And now it's got so much cheaper, it suddenly seemed possible. I've always wanted to see the Grand Canyon and Las Vegas.

Now act similar conversations in pairs between:
Mrs Crewe and a friend
Mick Silver and a friend
Nora Greene and a friend
Lucy Adams and a friend

Say when you're going, how long for, and give your reasons for choosing the holiday.

3

Mike has made a list of things to buy for his holiday. Here is part of the list:

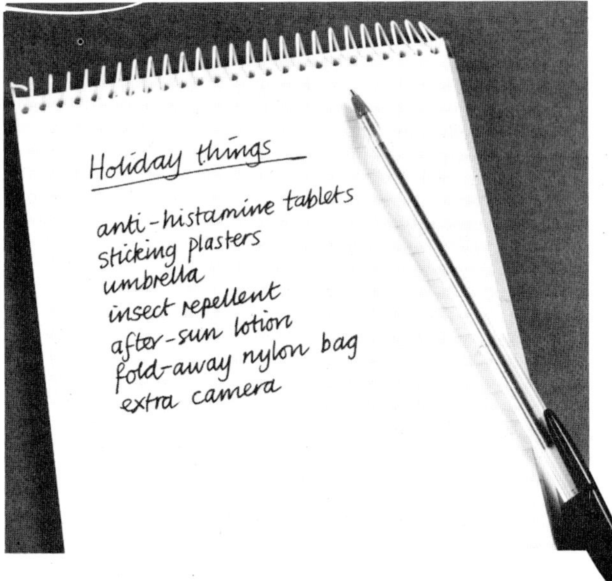

Mike explains the list to Pat:

MIKE: I need to get some anti-histamine tablets.
PAT: Really? What for?
MIKE: In case I get hay fever while I'm there.
PAT: Oh. Haven't you got any at home?
MIKE: No, I've run out of them.

Note: 'in case I get', *not* 'in case I will get'.

In pairs, act similar conversations about the other items on the list. Use these cues to help you:

MIKE: *Say what you want to buy.*
PAT: *Ask for reason.*
MIKE: *Give reason using 'in case'.*
PAT: *Check if item is really needed.*
MIKE: *Confirm need with reason.*

What else do you think you need to take with you on holiday abroad? E.g. passport, guide book, credit cards, phrase book.

I would	suggest recommend	taking . . . buying . . . getting . . .

Write five suggestions or recommendations in the same way. If you like, explain why, using in case . . .

4

Imagine you are Mike or Pat. Go into the chemist's and buy all the items that you need from there. One of you must be the shop assistant.

Here are some useful phrases:

PAT/MIKE:
Can I have a look at your selection of . . . ?
Have you got any . . . ?
Can you recommend anything for . . . ?
What sort of suntan lotion would you recommend for . . . ?

SHOP ASSISTANT:
What's it for exactly?
What sort of price did you have in mind?
Did you want a spray or a cream?

5

This is what happened to Mike and Pat when they left on their holiday.

MIKE: Oh no!
PAT: What's the matter?
MIKE: Look at that traffic jam! If it's like this all the way, we'll never get to the airport in time.
PAT: We should have left earlier.
MIKE: Yes, you're right.
PAT: Well, we'll just have to sit and wait. There's nothing we can do.

Act similar conversations for these situations. Use these phrases:

We / You should (n't) have . . .
Why did (n't) we / you . . .
If only we'd (hadn't) . . .
I wish you'd (hadn't) . . .

6

Mike and Pat are having a meal out in Las Vegas. The waitress brings them the bill.

MIKE: Oh, excuse me. I think there seems to be some mistake. We've been charged for two ice-cream sodas but we only had coffee.
GIRL: Oh, you have? I'm sorry, sir. I'll make you out a new check.
MIKE: Thanks.

In pairs, act out these situations:

(i) You have booked a room with a private bath at a hotel. When you get to the room you find that there is only a shower. Tell the receptionist.

(ii) You go into a newsagent and buy a newspaper and a magazine, costing 75p altogether. You give the shop assistant £1 but only get 15p change. Tell the shop assistant.

(iii) You have asked for a seat in the non-smoking area in the plane, but find yourself in a seat in the smoking area. Tell the air steward.

Report to a third person what happened in each case, like this:

'When we were in a restaurant in Las Vegas, we found that we had been overcharged so . . .'

7

Pat and Mike are shopping in San Francisco.

PAT: I like that T-shirt.
MIKE: Why don't we get one for your brother?
PAT: No, I'm not sure he'd ever wear it.

Make similar conversations. Use the table in the next column and the display of gifts below. Make suggestions for presents; approve or disapprove as you wish.

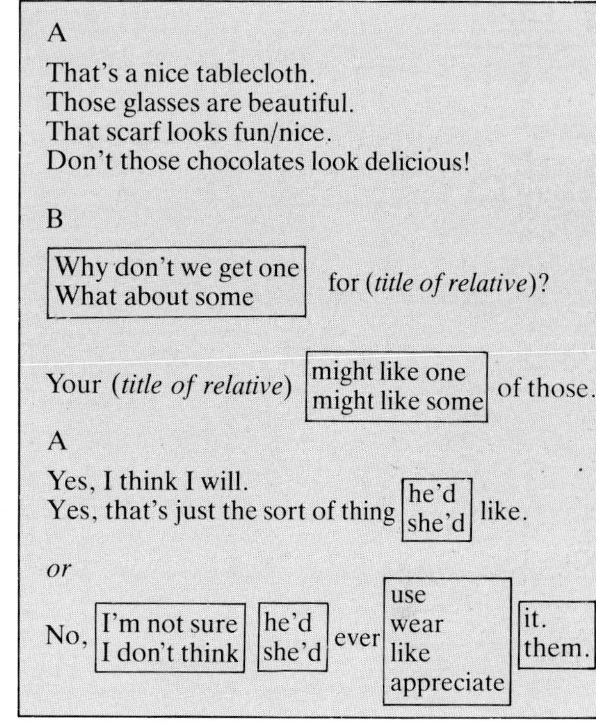

A

That's a nice tablecloth.
Those glasses are beautiful.
That scarf looks fun/nice.
Don't those chocolates look delicious!

B

Why don't we get one / What about some	for (*title of relative*)?

Your (*title of relative*)	might like one / might like some	of those.

A

Yes, I think I will.

Yes, that's just the sort of thing	he'd / she'd	like.

or

No,	I'm not sure / I don't think	he'd / she'd	ever	use / wear / like / appreciate	it. / them.

Think of a foreign country and list three things you might buy as presents for your friends and family at home. Tell your partner what presents you have bought, for whom and why, like this:

For my . . .

mother aunt nephew cousin neighbour sister-in-law	I would buy	a model of the Empire State Building some duty-free liqueur an ornament of some kind some example of the local crafts

because . . .

Jackie Wilson is the travel representative for the tour which Mike and Pat have joined. She is answering questions from different people on the telephone.

Read the information about the holiday, look at her answers and write down the questions that were asked, like this:

ANSWER (1): Yes, they are. And state taxes, too.
QUESTION: Are local taxes included in the price?

What's included

- *Round trip air travel London-New York and San Francisco-London by scheduled service wide-bodied jet.*
- *Trans-America air travel principally by United Airlines.*
- *Three nights in New York, including a half-day tour of Manhattan.*
- *Two nights in Washington, DC, including city tour.*
- *Two nights in Las Vegas, including Hoover Dam tour.*
- *Optional air tour to Grand Canyon.*
- *Three nights in Los Angeles and four nights in San Francisco, including city tour.*
- *State and local taxes.*
- *Membership of New York Dining Club.*
- *Holiday-planning kit.*

1. Yes, they are. And state taxes too.
2. Nothing. The kit is included in the whole price of the holiday.
3. No, you don't. It's a direct flight from San Francisco.
4. Two nights, sir, yes.
5. Oh yes, of course. We'll be doing a half-day tour.
6. No, you don't have to, but it's well worth seeing.

9 Listening

English has many varieties, for example, British English and American English. Listen to Jean, an American, talking about an incident that happened during her holiday. Look at the lists of words below and match the words that Jean uses in column 1 with the equivalent British English expressions in column 2.

Retell her story as a native British speaker would have told it.

American English	British English
highway	bonnet
vacation	toilets
hood	lorry
fender	motorway
gas	bumper
mobile/trailer home	holiday
truck	caravan
rest room	petrol

Los Angeles
Why not see *Disneyland* in a full day's visit to the fairytale wonderland of Walt Disney? Here's the chance to see the world of tomorrow or Sleeping Beauty's castle; view the mysterious underwater world from a submarine; investigate a haunted mansion; go on a jungle cruise; wander through New Orleans. You can ride a monorail, cable cars, a train straight from the American West or a Mississippi steamboat. You have a choice of tickets entitling you to eleven rides.

10 Trip to the States!

1. Where would you go for:
– a cowboy holiday?
– a rock-and-roll holiday?
– a cultural holiday?
– a fairy-tale holiday?
– a shopping holiday?
– an old-world holiday?
– a natural beauty holiday?
– an architectural elegance holiday?

New York! New York!

This city, often referred to as 'the Big Apple', has starred in a million movies and its skyline is the most famous in the world. Don't miss the Metropolitan, Guggenheim and Natural History museums; Greenwich Village, Wall Street and the Statue of Liberty. Best views are from the top of the Empire State Building, Staten Island Ferry (a 1-hour round trip for just a few cents) and the Cloisters in Fort Tryon Park. Shop at Macy's and Gimbels, window-shop at the excellent stores along Fifth Avenue.

Boston

Visit the cradle of the American Revolution.

From Boston to Washington DC, it is 719 km (450 miles). Along this narrow coastal strip more than 20% of the population live in less than 2% of the country's land area. Washington DC, at the southern end of this string of cities, has little industry and no skyscrapers. The Capitol, the White House, the Washington Monument and the Lincoln and Jefferson Memorials are the major landmarks.

Atlanta

Atlanta is a city of surprises. Look up at the typical American-skyscraper skyline of downtown Atlanta, dominated by the cylindrical Peachtree Plaza Hotel, which at 220 metres (723 feet) claims to be the tallest hotel in the world.

Then dip in Underground Atlanta, to the gaslit gaiety of the '90s, for this is surprising Atlanta where the new and the old live together happily.

New Orleans

The name of New Orleans conjures up images of jazz bands on Bourbon Street, Mardi Gras and Mississippi river boats. Go there and make your dreams come true!

The Grand Canyon

Don't forget 'the world's most wonderful spectacle': 396 km (277 miles) long, over 8 km (5 miles) wide and 1,609 metres (1 mile) deep. Take the Grand Canyon air trip for the experience of a life-time.

Nashville

Come to Nashville, Tennessee, the country and western music capital. See Elvis Presley's solid gold Cadillac.

Cheyenne Frontier Days Rodeo

Cheyenne, Wyoming: The oldest US rodeo and the granddaddy of them all is a long-standing tradition in Wyoming. In addition to the usual competitive events, there are night shows, featuring country and western performers and chuckwagon races. Last full week in July. Information: PO Box 2385, Cheyenne, WY 82001 (307 634-7794).

San Francisco

What will inspire you is the sight of the Golden Gate Bridge soaring across a blue and sunlit sea. Travel on a cable car up to Nob Hill, eat seafood overlooking the bay. Leave your heart in San Francisco.

2. Using the patterns suggested, write statements about the different places to visit in the United States.

One of the best views is from the Empire State Building, *from which* you can see the whole of the island of Manhattan.

Peachtree Plaza Hotel/whole of downtown Atlanta.
Cable cars in Disneyland/whole of the fairy-tale wonderland.

Don't miss the Guggenheim Museum, where you can find a unique collection of modern art.

Disneyland/ride a monorail, cable car or Mississippi steamboat.
Nashville, Tennessee/Elvis Presley's gold Cadillac.

New Orleans, the name *of which* conjures up images of jazz and Mississippi steamboats, is a popular tourist attraction.

Nashville/country and western music heroes.
Cheyenne, Wyoming/cowboys and rodeos.

Pat and Mike are keeping a journal of their holiday for their firm's newsletter.

DATELINE LAS VEGAS

We have just had our first breakfast in Las Vegas and we are sitting on our balcony overlooking a spectacular swimming pool. We can feel the sun getting hotter and hotter. How we managed to stay up half the night we don't know. It is probably due to the excitement of gambling for the first time - whether you approve of gambling or not.

The guide books say that Las Vegas is the greatest, most popular, most luxurious, most honest gambling centre the world has ever known. For once the guide books seem to be right, but I am not sure about the honesty!

What is interesting about Las Vegas is the fact it is a relatively 'young' city. It was founded as recently as 1905. Apparently in those early days it consisted of a vast area of desert, surrounded by deserted gold and silver mines. There were no natural resources. What single asset the state of Nevada had, however, was the attitude of its citizens: in a word, they were gamblers. Where you gamble is up to you. There is a wide choice but Las Vegas is psychologically a most dangerous place to visit. You see, the casinos are open twenty-four hours of the day; they provide free drinks, free food and free entertainment with the most popular stars of the world. They try to make gambling a pleasure.

Moreover, what is quite fascinating about the Vegas casinos is that there are no clocks visible anywhere. There is nothing to distract you from gambling. For when the gamblers lose, the casinos win!

Check

How did Pat and Mike manage to stay up half the night?
What is interesting about the history of Las Vegas?
What was the 'single asset' that the state of Nevada had?
What opinion in the guide books do Mike and Pat agree with?
What do Pat and Mike feel is so fascinating about the casinos?

Complete

First, in pairs, complete the sentences below and then write them out in your notebooks. Use the information on pages 10 and 11, like this:

What is most spectacular about the Grand Canyon is its size.

What we are most looking forward to seeing in San Francisco . . .
What is magic about Disneyland . . .
What you mustn't miss in Washington . . .
What music fans love about Nashville . . .
What is unusual about Atlanta . . .

Now write four or five sentences about your capital city, beginning in the same way with what. **Write about sightseeing, shopping, eating out, entertainment and things a visitor should not miss.**

Writing

(i) Imagine you are Pat or Mike. Write postcards to three friends or relatives from three different places marked on the map of the United States. Say how you are enjoying your holiday, what you have done and seen so far, your impressions of the place you are in, and your plans for the next few days. Use the photographs, texts and exercises to help you.

(ii) Think of a city, or a region which you know well, and write one or two paragraphs describing its attractions for a visitor.

Oral exercises

1. Expressing precautions

Simon is preparing to go on holiday. A friend, Alison, is giving him advice about what to take.

SIMON: Shall I take some aspirin?
ALISON: *Yes, I would, in case you get a headache.*

1. an international driving licence
2. some writing paper and some envelopes
3. an extra sweater
4. some fruit for the journey
5. a spare pair of glasses

2. Asking for recommendations

You are going shopping at the chemists. Ask for recommendations in the following situations:

You have dry hair. You want to buy some shampoo.
What sort of shampoo would you recommend for dry hair?

1. You have a sensitive skin. You want to buy some suntan lotion.
2. You have a Canon camera. You want to buy a colour film.
3. You have fine hair. You want to buy some shampoo.
4. You have an upset stomach. You want to buy some tablets.
5. Your baby has a bad cough. You want to buy some cough mixture.

3. Regretting actions

The Robinsons are on a long car journey, and all sorts of things have gone wrong.

MR ROBINSON: Why on earth didn't we buy an up-to-date map!
MRS ROBINSON: *Yes, if only we'd bought an up-to-date map, this would never have happened.*

1. I wish we hadn't taken so much luggage!
2. Why didn't we check the time of the ferry!
3. I wish we'd taken the car in for a proper service.
4. Why didn't we take the motorway!
5. It's a pity we forgot the spare fanbelt.

4. Focussing

A parent is not very happy about the life his son is leading now that he has left home.

FATHER: You seem to spend all your time in discos.
SON: *Look, how I spend my time is my business!*
FATHER: But where do you go every evening?
SON: *Look, where I go every evening is my business!*

1. You seem to spend all your time in discos.
2. But where do you go every evening?
3. Yes, but you should think what you do with your money.
4. I'm worried about what you are doing with your life.
5. Maybe, but I'm entitled to know who your friends are.
6. But I'm mostly concerned about where you go at the weekends.

Unit 1 Study focus

Interaction

FUNCTION	STRUCTURE
1. Expressing precaution	'in case' + present tense
2. Asking about availability in shops	'Have you got any/anything for . . .?'
3. Asking for recommendation in shops	'recommend' something for NP
4. Giving recommendation	'suggest/recommend' + (ing)
5. Regretting and/or blaming others for past actions	'if only' + past perfect 'I wish' + past perfect 'should(n't) have' + past participle
6. Complaining in service situations	'seems to be . . .' 'We've been charged/sold . . .'
7. Making, accepting and rejecting suggestions about gifts, with reasons	'I'm not sure/don't think he/she'd ever wear/use . . .'

ADDITIONAL STRUCTURES

1. present and past perfect passive
2. relative, non-defining clauses introduced by 'of/from which/where'
3. sentences introduced by a 'What/where/how/why' clause.

Vocabulary

Travel and touring
British and American English

Writing skills

1. Three holiday postcards
2. Paragraph writing: describing tourist features

Unit 2 It could happen to anyone!

Before you start:

Have you ever lost anything valuable?
Was it stolen or did you just lose it?
What did you do about it?
If you saw a stranger climbing in through the window of a neighbour's house, what would you do?

Birchwood Centre is a further education centre in Maidstone, Kent. It provides young people who have just left school with special professional training in subjects such as accountancy,

hairdressing, secretarial skills and computer programming. The students usually work from nine to four-thirty, with an hour off for lunch. Most students have lunch in the refectory at the Centre.

This is what happened to Marilyn Barker, a young student on the computer studies course, one day last week.

Follow the pictures and tell the story.

1.

You are Marilyn. Talk to Bob Arnold, the caretaker at Birchwood Centre.

BOB: What's the matter? You look very worried!
MARILYN: . . . .
BOB: No, nobody has handed one in. What does it look like?
MARILYN: . . . .
BOB: I see. What was inside it?
MARILYN: . . . .
BOB: Was there any form of identity in it? Anything with your name on it?
MARILYN: . . . .
BOB: Good. Well, if anyone hands it in, I'll let you know right away.
MARILYN: . . . .
BOB: And don't worry. It's bound to turn up.

Practise the conversation again in pairs. This time you have lost your **handbag or wallet.**

Make a similar notice to Marilyn's about your handbag or wallet.

2. Listening

Later in the afternoon, Marilyn tells the Principal about her missing shoulder bag. Two other students, Lee and Kelly, have also lost some valuable items. They also tell the Principal about them.

Listen to the conversation between Marilyn and the Principal, Mrs Hardwick. Write down the details missing from the chart below.

Listen to the conversation again and note down the questions which Mrs Hardwick asked Marilyn.

3. Use these questions and the information in the chart about the other missing items, and roleplay the conversations between Mrs Hardwick and Lee, and Mrs Hardwick and Kelly.

NAME	Item missing	Description	Last seen	Noticed missing
Marilyn Barker	shoulder bag	brown leather with large buckle Contains purse, keys, address book, letter		
Lee Franklin	wallet	black, imitation leather. Contains student union card, train season ticket, £5, 2 tickets for pop concert	left in jacket pocket in cloakroom before lunch	after lunch about 1.30 – wanted to go to shops
Kelly Edwards	watch	square, gold plated, Swiss, Roman figures, white leather strap	in ladies before lunch – took it off to wash and forgot to put it on	about 2.00. Went back to ladies but no sign of watch

4. Mrs Hardwick decides to call the police. Write down her conversation with a police officer from Maidstone Police Station, following these cues.

POLICE OFFICER: *Answer the phone. Ask if you can help.*
MRS HARDWICK: *Say who you are.*
POLICE OFFICER: *Ask what the trouble is.*
MRS HARDWICK: *Tell the police officer that some articles of value have been reported missing by some students and that you suspect they may have been stolen.*
POLICE OFFICER: *Ask why she suspects this.*
MRS HARDWICK: *Explain why.*
POLICE OFFICER: *Ask exactly what has been stolen.*
MRS HARDWICK: *Give information.*
POLICE OFFICER: *Suggest that you go to the Centre immediately and look into the matter further.*
MRS HARDWICK: *Thank the police officer and say that you'll be waiting in your office.*

Now act out the conversation in pairs.

5. Discuss who you think may have stolen the articles. Use phrases like:

It may / could / must have been taken by . . .

2 Burglary has become a massive industry. Businessmen who appear to be totally respectable place the orders for goods to be stolen - from paintings and antiques to wine and chocolate; receivers act as the middle men, placing the orders with suitable burglars; and the whole cycle often ends with unsuspecting members of the public purchasing the stolen goods - sometimes in High Street shops.

Check

Identify the people who:
- place the orders for goods to be stolen.
- commission the burglars. (The people who . . . are . . .)
- steal the goods.
- buy the goods.

Identify the goods which are often stolen.
Identify the places where the goods are sometimes sold.

Muriel

Muriel's home was a pleasant three-bedroomed detached house in a suburb of Manchester. The family, consisting of two girls and a boy, had been raised there. One had already left home, and the day was not far off when the other two would leave for London and the start of their careers.

The house now lacked for nothing. The expensive days of schooling and providing for a growing family were over. The husband's salary as an engineer provided holidays in Spain, a year-old family car, a colour television (not rented now, thanks to a bargain offer in a January sale), and the lounge even boasted a corner with a 'bar', complete with two stools.

Life was good until Muriel, returning from a shopping expedition in the city centre, found she has been burgled. It was bad enough that the French windows in the rear dining-room had been forced open and £20 in cash in the kitchen drawer stolen; but the damage and vandalism aged Muriel on the spot, inflicting a mental wound even time would not heal.

A booted foot had shattered the television screen, leaving smashed glass, dangling wires and a jumble of crushed miniature valves. The three-piece suite had been up-ended and the fabric slashed – possibly in the hope that money had been hidden inside. Houseplants had been torn from their pots and hurled against walls. There was a horror in the kitchen. Three fish were dead on the floor, their heads stamped and crushed; they were from the family's small aquarium. The actual fish tank was not broken – it was constructed of tough plastic – but it had been knocked from its stand and the water had soaked the fitted carpet. Kitchen drawers had been yanked out and the contents strewn over the floor.

It was the same story in each room: devastation. Muriel found she could not sleep. The extra sherry at night did not work. The doctor later prescribed tranquillizers. Ultimately her husband made the only decision he could. They had to sell and move from the home where they had planned to spend the rest of their lives.

The tragedy is that each year there are many thousands of Muriels.

from *The Burglary Business and You* by Peter Burden

1. When Muriel realised what had happened, she telephoned her husband, Ron. Fill in Muriel's side of the conversation from information in the text and supply the correct form of the verbs in brackets. Write out the complete conversation afterwards and read it in pairs.

MURIEL: Ron, something awful (happen). We (burgle).
RON: Oh no! When?
MURIEL: Just this morning. They (must/get) in while . . . .
RON: What they (take)?
MURIEL: Well, they only (take) . . . as far as I can see. It's not that – oh Ron, you should just see what the house looks like.
RON: What they (do)?
MURIEL: The place is just completely upside-down. They . . . . the TV set; they . . . . . . the furniture and the material . . . . They (must/think) . . . . And the walls are in a terrible mess because they . . . .
RON: Is it only the lounge?
MURIEL: No, everywhere! The bedrooms, the dining-room – and the kitchen! They (kill) the goldfish. The aquarium was too . . . . .for them to break but the carpet . . . . .and the floor (cover) with . . . .
RON: How they (get in)?
MURIEL: They (must get) into the . . . . .by . . . . .the French windows.
RON: You (report) it to the police?
MURIEL: No. I (do) it now.

2. Before going to the police station, Muriel made a note of everything that had been stolen or damaged, like this. Complete the list.

£20 stolen
French windows forced
TV screen . . . .
Furniture fabric . . . .
Houseplants . . . . .and . . . .
Fish . . . . .and . . . .
Carpet . . . .
Kitchen drawers . . . .
Contents . . . .

Word study

(i) Group the words which are similar in meaning. Underline the words which sound violent.

pull	yank	flatten	hurl	smash
spread	mark	soak	fling	throw
slash	strew	tread on	crush	break
saturate	rip	pull apart	tear	dampen
scatter	stain	squash	stamp on	shatter

(ii) How could you damage the following objects? Match possible verbs from the list above with the object(s).

armchair	flowers	wallpaper	telephone
books	curtains	vase	pictures
carpet	window	record-player	

Discuss

Why was the Muriel incident particularly sad?
Why do you think the burglars vandalised the house?
Does vandalism occur in your home town?

Writing

Write Muriel's letter to a friend in which she explains briefly about the burglary, what she and Ron did about it, how she felt, what the doctor has said, what is happening now and how they have finally decided to move.

1. Look at the picture of the sitting room. Describe the room and the furniture in it.

2. Imagine some burglars have broken into the house and caused a lot of damage. Say what has happened to the following:

The sofa has been . . .	The roses . . .
The curtains have been . . .	The lamp . . .
The chairs . . .	The coffee table . . .
The television . . .	The books . . .
The vase . . .	The carpet . . .
	The hi-fi . . .

3. Using this information, complete the following advertisement for a burglar alarm.

For weeks everything felt dirty. When I got back one evening after a hard time shopping with the children, I was looking forward to a cup of tea and a doze. Imagine the horror I felt when I was greeted by a wrecked and vandalised house. In the sitting room . . .
I can see now that I had been foolish. If only I had taken the advice of our friends and bought a Century Burglar Protection System .

Listening

A man whose house has been burgled is explaining to the insurance representative what has been taken. Number the pictures below in the order in which they are mentioned and write a caption (short description) for each item.

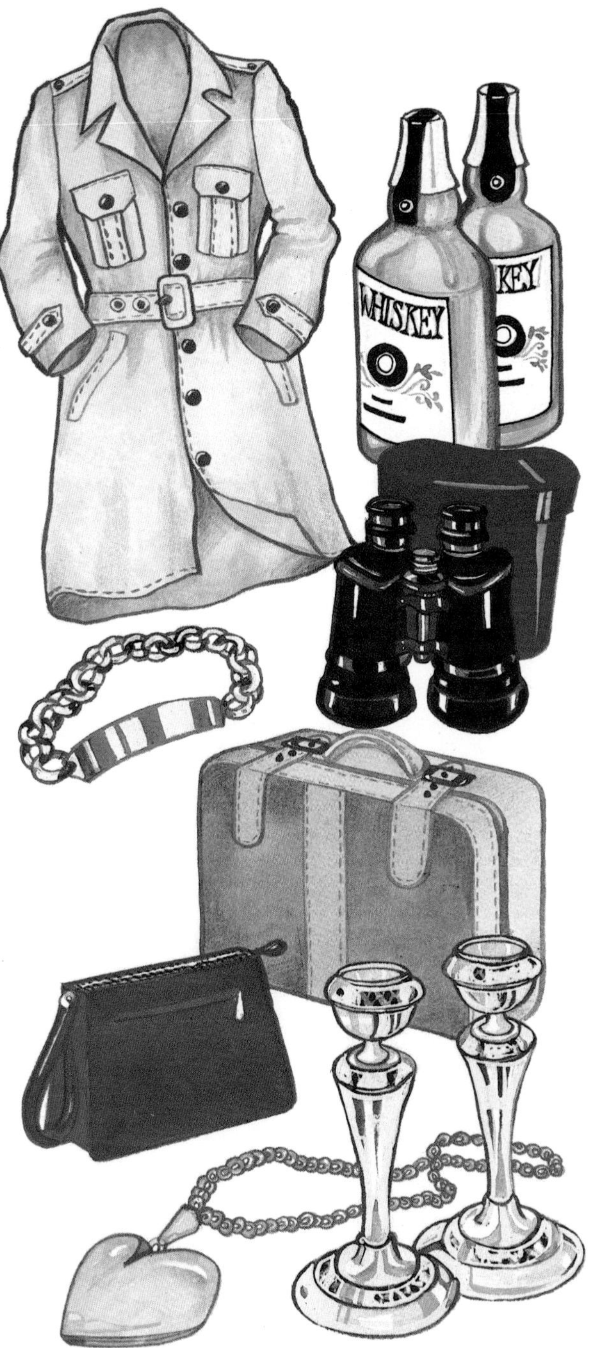

Word study

(i) Look at the following items and say where on your body or clothes you would wear them:

locket	bangle	brooch	pendant
crucifix	chain	necklace	bracelet
earrings	cufflinks	string of pearls	ring

(ii) Divide the following into metals and stones. Decide which are precious and which are semi-precious:

silver	ruby	gold	diamond
amethyst	platinum	opal	sapphire
emerald	jet	amber	bronze

Now use one of those words to describe people in each of these sentences:
Her eyes sparkled like . . .
Her lips were . . .red.
His hair was . . .black.
She wore a simple . . .blue evening dress.
Her green blouse matched the . . .of her eyes.
Her hair shone like . . .in the morning sun.

(iii) Imagine that a local jewellery shop has been burgled. Make an inventory of six items of jewellery that have been stolen.

5

An open letter to a trio of thieves

This is an open letter to the three people who stole my handbag from the Highgate boutique where I am employed as a sales assistant.

When you took my bag I don't know what you thought you were going to get. With my wages, there's not much left on a Tuesday. I hope the £5 was useful to you. I have informed the social security office so you won't be able to cash the child benefit next week. I hope that won't leave you too short, but if you really need a couple of pounds, I suppose you could always cash one of the two cheques left in my cheque book. Of course, I phoned the bank right away and the cheque-cashing card is no longer valid, so it won't be much use to you.

Actually I don't mind about the money too much. We single parents who work to support our families understand only too well what it means to be short of cash. However, I don't suppose it went very far between three of you. Sorry about that!

I wish you had left the bag behind and just taken the wallet and cheque book. There were all kinds of papers in it, and notes and things that I really need. I really think that was very inconsiderate of you. I mean, how would you like something like that to happen to you?

Well, perhaps the bag will turn up. It wasn't even an expensive one, just a plain, old brown leather shoulder bag. You probably dumped it in the nearest rubbish bin or threw it over the park railings into the bushes. We've looked around, of course, but no-one saw which way you went after you left the shop.

I'm not really angry with you. I know how the pressures of modern living can affect one, but I am sad and distressed at the loss of my personal things. I feel violated and helpless, and although the police were very nice, they just shrugged their shoulders. 'It happens all the time,' they told me. Some small comfort, I suppose. But I've lost just a little more faith in human nature. And as my young son said when I told him what had happened, 'Why, Mummy, why us?' I couldn't answer that question. I wonder if you can?

Louise B. Raphael,
Southwood Avenue,
Highgate, N6.

1. Complete the following information:

Article stolen:
Description:
Contents:
Where stolen:
Owner:
Job:
Family status:

2. What items in the handbag did Ms Raphael consider more important to her than her money?

Look through your own handbag or wallet. List in two columns what are valuable **items, and what are** important but not valuable **items.**

3. Which three of your personal possessions would you be most sad or distressed at losing?

6 Listening

Listen to this person talking about a burglary at his house. Note down as you listen:

What was taken:
What damage was done:
How the burglar broke in:
What he did about it:

Writing

Write a composition which starts: 'It could happen to anyone. I had decided to spend the day in . . .' and ends: 'My life has never been the same since.'

Oral exercises

1. Describing things

Have you seen my handbag? It's black. And it's made of leather.
Yes, I saw a black leather handbag a few moments ago.

1. wallet / brown / made of pigskin
2. briefcase / dark brown / made of leather
3. holdall / big / red / made of nylon
4. umbrella / black / telescopic
5. shoulder bag / large / embroidered
6. file / green / made of plastic

2. Describing damage

Did they really ruin the carpets?
Yes, they've been completely ruined.

1. smash – mirror
2. wreck – kitchen
3. soak – carpet
4. tear – wallpaper
5. damage – hi-fi system
6. ruin – sofa

3. Describing the scene after a burglary

Look at the TV!
It's been totally smashed!

I can't find the silver candlesticks anywhere.
So they've been stolen, then.

1. Look at the crystal vase!
2. I can't find my gold bracelet.
3. Have you seen the housekeeping money anywhere? I can't see it.
4. Oh no! Look at that window!
5. Just look at those glasses!
6. I can't find my jewellery anywhere.
7. I can't seem to find my camera. I've looked everywhere!

4. Drawing conclusions

Some valuable items are missing at college.

I think I'll ask the secretary about my handbag.
Yes, it could have been handed in. (possibility)

Nobody's seen my wallet. I've asked everyone.
Well, it must have been stolen, then. (inference)

1. I'll go and ask the caretaker if he's seen my books.
2. Perhaps the secretary's got my ID card.
3. I can't find my watch anywhere.
4. I've asked everyone about my wallet and no-one's seen it.
5. Maybe the secretary has got my gloves.

Unit 2 Study focus

Interaction

FUNCTION	STRUCTURE
1. Reporting and explaining loss of personal property	present perfect, past simple
2. Describing personal property	present tense
3. Drawing conclusions (possibility and inference)	'may' 'might have (been)' . . . 'must'
4. Describing damaged condition	passive tenses: present and past perfect, past simple

ADDITIONAL STRUCTURES
1. word order of adjectives
2. defining relative clauses with 'who/which/whose'

Vocabulary

Personal possessions
Adjectives of size, colour, material and type
Verbs to do with vandalism and violence
House interiors: furniture and fittings
Jewellery: semi-precious and precious metals and stones

Writing skills

1. Notice: lost property
2. Note-taking from conversation and text
3. Informal letter: narration and description
4. Paragraph writing (for advertisement): narration and description
5. Descriptive captions
6. Inventory of stolen jewellery
7. Composition: narration and description

Unit 3 People in our lives

Age and physical appearance	Personal qualities: how you feel and behave
Family background	Job interests and achievements
Domestic life	

Before you start:

You want to know about a person. What questions do you ask to get the information shown in the diagram above? E.g. How old is she?

1

Match each person below with their descriptions in the notes.

NAME	GAVIN	MARIA	LYNSEY	GORDON
Occupation	dog breeder	solicitor	bus driver	teacher
Height	tall	medium	short	tall
Build	thickset	slim	well-built	slim, athletic
Hair	red, wiry	long, auburn	short Afro	straight, fair
Eyes	blue	grey-green	brown	hazel
Skin	tanned, freckled	olive	black	fair
Special feature	thick, red beard	mole on cheek	glasses	low, husky voice
Clothes and accessories	sweater, corduroy trousers, boots, big belts	smart, well cut, gold necklaces	off duty: bright, inexpensive fashionable	bomber jacket, T-shirts, jeans

After a party

S1: What did you think of Lynsey?
S2: Which one was Lynsey?
S1: She was the bus driver.
S2: Oh, was she the one with the short Afro hair style and glasses?
S1: Yes, that's right. She was wearing a bright pink trouser suit.
S2: Oh yes. I thought she was rather nice.

1. In pairs, make similar conversations about the other three people. Use the notes and your own ideas.

2. Write about the people in the illustrations below, like this:

(i) Gavin is a dog breeder. He is tall and thickset with red, wiry hair. He has blue eyes, a tanned, freckled skin and a thick, red beard. He usually wears thick sweaters, corduroy trousers and boots because he has to work outside.

(ii) Gavin is a man . . .
. . .*whose* job involves working outside a lot.
. . .*whose* usual dress is a sweater, corduroy trousers and boots.

(iii) Gavin is a dog breeder . . .
. . .*which* means that he has to work outside a lot.
Maria has long, auburn hair . . .
. . .*which* she often wears tied back.

Write about two or three people you know in the same way.

3. Descriptions of people can be made more interesting . . .

Mr Goodall is a jolly man in his early fifties with a round, cheerful face. His twinkling blue eyes crease up and almost disappear when he smiles, which he does frequently. He is large and quite stout but speaks in a surprisingly gentle and soft manner.

Make a list of the words and expressions which you think add interest to the physical description of Mr Goodall, e.g. jolly.

4. Write a similar paragraph about a young man. Use these notes:

Name:	Gareth
Age:	late teens
Face:	serious, pale
Eyes:	grey, intelligent – somehow have a haunting, mysterious quality
Voice:	speaks slowly, with a husky, surprisingly deep voice

2

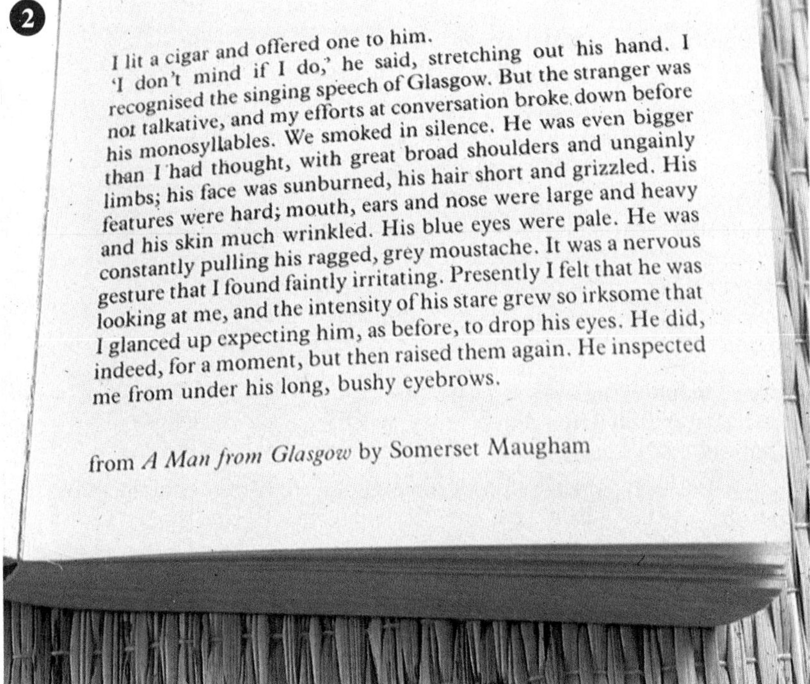

I lit a cigar and offered one to him.
'I don't mind if I do,' he said, stretching out his hand. I recognised the singing speech of Glasgow. But the stranger was not talkative, and my efforts at conversation broke down before his monosyllables. We smoked in silence. He was even bigger than I had thought, with great broad shoulders and ungainly limbs; his face was sunburned, his hair short and grizzled. His features were hard; mouth, ears and nose were large and heavy and his skin much wrinkled. His blue eyes were pale. He was constantly pulling his ragged, grey moustache. It was a nervous gesture that I found faintly irritating. Presently I felt that he was looking at me, and the intensity of his stare grew so irksome that I glanced up expecting him, as before, to drop his eyes. He did, indeed, for a moment, but then raised them again. He inspected me from under his long, bushy eyebrows.

from *A Man from Glasgow* by Somerset Maugham

1. What do you remember about the man from Glasgow? Without reading the passage again, list a few points, like this:
– quiet

2. Now read the passage again. List all the words and phrases which make the man seem unique and special, like this:

– the singing speech of Glasgow
– not talkative
– his monosyllables

3. Which words and phrases describe:
the man's accent?
his manner and personality?
his build and appearance?
his unconscious habits?

Example:
accent: singing speech of Glasgow
manner and personality: not talkative

4. Look at your list of words and phrases again. Make a note of those which show a positive or negative attitude on the part of the author, like this:

ungainly limbs negative

Writing

Think of a person you would like to write about. List the details of the person's appearance and personality you would like to mention, as in **3.** Make a special note of positive or negative feelings you would like to express, as in **4**. Write a short paragraph describing the person.

❸ Personal qualities

Personality quiz. Ask and answer in pairs.

Do you find it difficult to talk to strangers?
Do you think you are easy to get on with?
Do you like the idea of foreign travel?
Do you like to check things over and over again?
Do you get upset when people criticise you?
Do you find it difficult to look at insects, worms and blood?
Do you get irritated when people are late?
Do you refuse to accept other people's points of view?
Do you sometimes feel in a good mood and sometimes in a bad one?
Do you often say the wrong thing at the wrong time?

Match the following adjectives with the appropriate question:
adventurous tactless intolerant sensitive squeamish
impatient shy easy-going thorough moody

Change partners and ask the questions again, this time using the adjective, like this:
Are you shy?

❹ Matchmaker

● **MY IDEAL LADY** slim, attractive, long hair (waist-length), non-smoker, warm, caring and affectionate. If you are around, I am an attractive businessman, 39, own home with pool. Photo appreciated. All letters answered. Box P829.

● **ATTRACTIVE 29 YR-OLD BACHELOR** professional, HONEST, KIND, loves music, sport, outdoor life, seeks HONEST, WARM, SINCERE female to share experiences. Photo/phone if possible. Box M638.

● **ATTRACTIVE INTELLIGENT** professional girl (32) seeks similar tall, unattached man under 40, sincere, sense of humour, articulate, for genuine long-term relationship. Box P898.

● **ATTRACTIVE LADY** Young 45, warm, sensitive, interested in people, music, enjoying life; seeks intelligent, open, unattached man for caring, honest relationship. Box M751.

● **MALE 31,** graduate, shy, reasonable looks, seeks quiet, attractive, sincere girl. Interests include literature, music, mathematics, sport. Box P827.

● **SUCCESSFUL** young company director, good-looking, intelligent, ARTICULATE, KIND, wants to meet attractive girl, romantic enough to enjoy being kissed. You are adventurous, aware and willing TO BREAK ROUTINES. Photos unnecessary. Box P828

1. Read the 'small ads'. Which are from women looking for men? Which are from men looking for women? Choose three to study. Make notes on the qualities mentioned in the advertisements, like this:

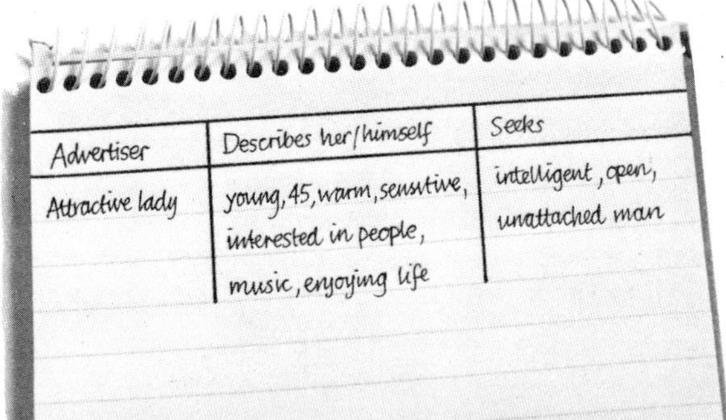

Advertiser	Describes her/himself	Seeks
Attractive lady	young, 45, warm, sensitive, interested in people, music, enjoying life	intelligent, open, unattached man

2. My ideal match is someone who is . . .

able to cook
generous
tolerant
educated
from a good family
sensitive
broadminded
attractive
from the same background
good with children
adventurous
warm
witty
sincere
intelligent
a non-smoker
interested in the same things as me
adaptable
the same age as me
well-off
affectionate
articulate
kind to animals
extrovert

In groups, say whether you think that each quality is very, rather **or** not important **to you.**

Find out the five qualities which most people think are very **important and two qualities which most people think are** not **important in a partner.**

❺ Star qualities

The following text comes from a popular book about astrology. To which sign do you think the text is referring?

Positive qualities

Patience, generosity, and sensitivity are the most outstanding qualities of people born under this sign. They are broad-minded and tolerant, and they have a wonderful capacity for quietly and tactfully dealing with others. They are honest, thorough and adaptable, and are capable of taking care of themselves. They are warm, sincere and have a good sense of humour. They are intelligent, articulate and generally well-informed on a wide variety of subjects, with a strong appreciation of music, literature and art. They are aware of the world about them.

Word study

Study these words of quality from the text and find the other related parts of speech:

patience	tolerant	adaptable
generosity	tactfully	warm
sensitivity	honest	sincere

Fill in a chart, like this:

ADJECTIVE	NOUN	ADVERB	OPPOSITE ADJECTIVE
patient	patience	patiently	impatient

Now find in the text the opposites to these words:

narrow-minded cold mean stupid careless ignorant

❻ Listening

John and Pat with their baby daughter, Jessica, have recently moved to the country. Sandra, a friend of Pat's, comes to visit them one evening. Listen to the conversation. Make brief notes in order to discuss the behaviour and the personalities of the people involved.

Writing

Write two or three paragraphs describing the qualities of someone you know, mentioning both their positive and negative qualities. Here are some ways of contrasting good and bad qualities:

Although he/she is rather . . . / very . . . / extremely . . .

he/she can, however, also be extremely . . . / very . . . / rather . . .

In spite of being . . ., he/she is . . .
Sometimes he/she is very . . ., but on the other hand, he/she is . . .
He/she is . . . . However, he/she . . .
He/she is . . . . Nevertheless, he/she . . .

7 Sting

Some years ago, Gordon Sumner dropped out of teaching to risk all in the chancy world of pop music. Two years later he was struggling to pay the rent. Now he's known as Sting, lead singer of today's hottest band, The Police, and he's a superstar. How did this ex-schoolmaster manufacture the right sound, the right image, the right brand of sex appeal, to make himself into a teenage idol? Lulu Appleton reports.

Gordon Sumner is an exceptionally good-looking man, idolised by millions and so rich he can afford all he could ever wish for. Better known as Sting, he's the lead singer of The Police. His naturally fair hair has replaced the dyed blond hair of his stage act. But still the face magnetises – the voice is low and husky, the eyes are bright and intelligent, yet wary.

Suddenly Sting has become a superstar. 'I can't walk down a street any more without feeling that people are watching me. I can't be anonymous any longer, and that's a drag,' he says.

'When I'm not working, all I want to do is revert to being a normal person. I make a point of walking round the streets, just being myself.'

'I'm fairly narcissistic,' he admits candidly, 'but my feet are on the ground. I've got a 13-year-old VW and a motorbike. I could have a large Rolls-Royce, but I don't need one. I'm just as shrewd about money as I ever was, and I've never been a spendthrift. On the other hand, if I really like something and want it, then the cost is unimportant.'

He and Frances bought the house in Ireland when Sting returned from The Police's highly successful world tour.

'I picked Ireland because, apart from being pleasant, you can stay in touch with England while enjoying life at a slower pace!' He also has Irish ancestry, and an Irish wife, Frances Tomelty, an established actress.

Physically, Sting and Frances are quite different. Where he is fair-haired and highly strung, she is dark and serene with a quiet charm. Seeing them together it is hard to imagine anything splitting them up. They are bound together – despite their differences – by a mutual respect and shared expectations.

Sting is very much a man of the Eighties: 'Frances refuses to be considered as merely my wife, which I'm glad about. She has her own career, she's ambitious and talented, but she has never let it affect her. It's always been that way. When we got married and had Joseph,' explains Sting, 'we both agreed that being parents was not going to affect our careers.'

A stable family life is obviously important to Sting. It remains the one constant factor in a world that has changed utterly for him since he gave up a career in teaching for the music business. Sting loved teaching, but could not resist the lure of playing in bands. So he tried to do both, teaching by day, playing by night, and snatching a few hours' sleep in between. It left him so exhausted that he knew he had to choose one or the other.

On the one hand he saw himself teaching for ever, perhaps ending up as a deputy headmaster. The other side of the coin was less predictable, but he chose it, armed only with tremendous self-confidence and determination.

He has succeeded in his original ambition to provide thoughtful, intelligent pop music, making The Police the most widely accepted band since the Beatles.

'But,' he concludes, 'money hasn't made me any happier than before. The money makes things easier and more convenient, but there are frustrations too. Always another hill to climb, and not just climb, but get to the top.'

1. In pairs, read the article about Sting. Make notes under the headings:

Physical appearance:
Personal qualities:
Background:
Domestic life:
Attitude to money:
Ambition:
Attitude to fame:

2. Use the following questions to roleplay an interview with Sting:

How do you see yourself?
What did you do before you became a pop star?
Why did you leave your job?
What sort of life do you have offstage?
Do you have any conflicts in your private life?
Why did you choose Ireland as a place to live?
What do you feel about being rich?
What is your artistic ambiton?
What is it like being famous?

8 Writing

Describe a person you like and admire. Use these headings:
physical appearance; clothes; personal qualities; family background; job and interests and achievements.
Start like this:
'A person I like and admire very much is | my . . .' / the . . .'

❾ People in fiction

David Herbert Lawrence – novelist, playwright and poet – was born at 8a Victoria Street, Eastwood, in Nottinghamshire, on 11th September, 1885. This mining town, its surroundings and its people, played an influential role in Lawrence's work. He frequently returned to his early background in his novels.

In this extract from his novel *Sons and Lovers* (1913), Lawrence describes a scene between Mr Morel, a pit worker, and his wife and children, especially his young son, Paul.

He was shut out from all family affairs. No one told him anything. The children, alone with their mother, told her all about the day's happenings, everything. Nothing had really taken place in them until it was told to their mother. But as soon as the father came in, everything stopped. He was like the scotch in the smooth, happy machinery of the home. And he was always aware of this fall of silence on his entry, the shutting off of life, the unwelcome. But now it was gone too far to alter.

He would dearly have liked the children to talk to him, but they could not. Sometimes Mrs Morel would say: 'You ought to tell your father.'

Paul won a prize in a competition in a child's paper. Everybody was highly jubilant.

'Now you'd better tell your father when he comes in,' said Mrs Morel. 'You know how he carries on and says he's never told anything.'

'All right,' said Paul. But he would almost rather have forfeited the prize than have to tell his father.

'I've won a prize in a competition, Dad,' he said.

Morel turned round to him.

'Have you, my boy? What sort of a competition?'

'Oh nothing – about famous women.'

'And how much is the prize, then, as you've got?'

'It's a book.'

'Oh, indeed!'

'About birds.'

'Hm – hm!'

And that was all. Conversation was impossible between the father and any other member of the family. He was an outsider.

The only times when he entered again into the life of his own people was when he worked, and was happy at work. Sometimes, in the evening, he cobbled the boots or mended the kettle or his pit-bottle. Then he always wanted several attendants, and the children enjoyed it. They united with him in the work, in the actual doing of something, when he was his real self again.

1. Complete these statements:

The children rarely talked
- to their mother
- to their father
- to each other.

Mr Morel liked most of all
- to relax
- to talk
- to work.

The relationship between Paul and his father was
- distant
- loving
- friendly

2. Which four **of these words and phrases from the text are associated directly with Mr Morel?**

unwelcome	shut out
outsider	famous
jubilant	fall of silence

3. How did Mr Morel react to
- Paul winning a competition?
- Paul's prize?

4. *Sons and Lovers* is partly autobiographical. Lawrence is describing the relationships between himself (Paul Morel) and his family.

Do you know any other writers whose work is at least partly autobiographical?

Oral exercises

1. Identifying people

A friend is reminding you of people you met at a party.

Do you remember Mr Goodall?
Yes, wasn't he a gardener?
That's right.
Yes, I remember him. He had grey hair and twinkling blue eyes, didn't he?

Look at the people on page 22 and talk about them in the same way. Mention their occupations and special features.

Extra work
Re-express the answers, like this:
Yes, I remember him. He was the one who had grey hair and twinkling blue eyes.

2. Discussing personal qualities (1)

I like people to be generous.
Yes, I think generosity is important too.

1. sensitive
2. punctual
3. sincere
4. adaptable
5. original
6. reliable

3. Discussing personal qualities (2)

Andrea is talking about the personal qualities of her friend, Joe, with her flatmate, Lucy.

A: The trouble is, Joe isn't exactly tolerant.
L: *Well, tolerance isn't everything, you know.*

1. kind
2. attractive
3. articulate
4. patient
5. intelligent

Extra work
Re-express Lucy's comments, like this:
I agree. He is rather intolerant.

4. Discussing personal qualities (3)

I don't find Mandy very sensitive.
I agree. But she seems to have lots of friends in spite of being insensitive.

1. kind
2. patient
3. tolerant
4. sincere
5. intelligent
6. imaginative

Extra work
Re-express the answers, like this:
Yes, I agree. She acts rather insensitively at times.

Unit 3 Study focus

Interaction

FUNCTION	STRUCTURE
1. Identifying people	'Which one was . . . ?' 'Was he/she the one with . . . ?' 'He was the one who . . .'
2. Discussing appearance	'She had . . .' 'She was wearing . . .'
3. Discussing personal qualities	negative adjective prefixes: 'un', 'in' noun suffixes: 'ness', 'ity', 'ce'
4. Making concessions and contrasts	'in spite of', 'nevertheless', 'although', 'however', 'sometimes', 'on the other hand'
5. Modifying qualities	'extremely', 'rather', 'very'

ADDITIONAL STRUCTURES
1. defining relative clauses 'whose'
2. non-defining relative clauses 'which'
3. adverbs with negative prefix 'unimaginatively', 'insincerely'

Vocabulary
Clothes and accessories
Physical features
Personal qualities: positive and negative

Writing skills
1. Guided paragraphs: describing physical appearance
2. Note-taking from advertisements
3. Composition about a person you know well
4. Note-taking from a magazine article

Unit 4 Accident on the A24

Before you start:

What causes car accidents? Think of the following:
- weather and road conditions
- the condition of the car
- the condition of the driver.

1 Listening

Dr Denis James is a family doctor. He lives in Dorking, Surrey, with his wife, Helen, and their three children. He works with a group of General Practitioners. They take it in turns to be on call at the weekend. On Saturday, 14th November, Dr James is on duty. At quarter-past seven in the evening, the telephone rings at his home.

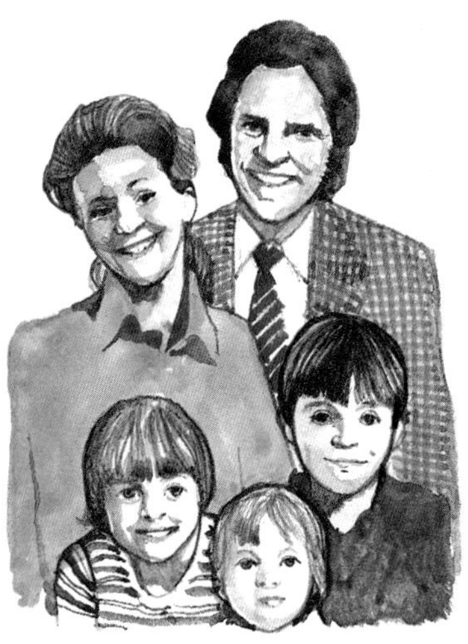

1. Listen to the conversation and:
- write down the name and address of the patient whom Dr James must go and visit.
- on the map on the right, mark the place where the patient lives.
- report what the person on the phone said about the patient and what he asked the doctor to do.

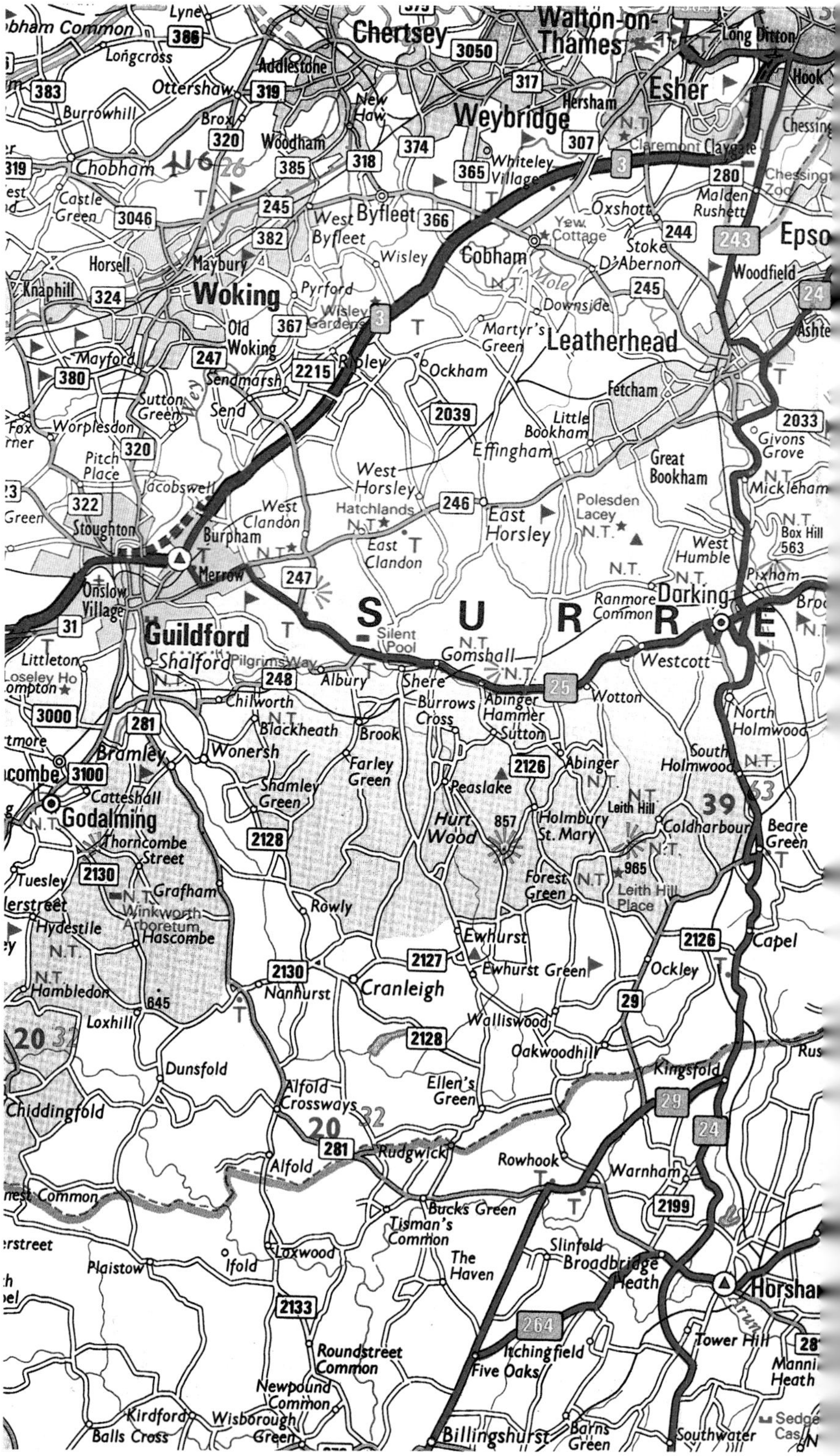

© 1981 George Philip & Son Ltd

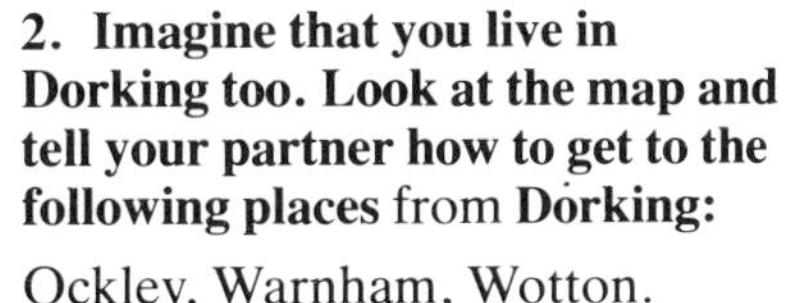

2. Imagine that you live in Dorking too. Look at the map and tell your partner how to get to the following places from **Dorking:**

Ockley, Warnham, Wotton.

These phrases may help you:

Take the A24 as far as . . .
Turn left/right down the A25
Drive past/round/over the . . .
You'll see a . . . on your left/right

Dr James leaves a message for his wife, Helen, who is out at a meeting.

7.20pm

Helen,
I've just had a call to go and see a patient in Capel. I don't expect I'll be back before 9.30 or 10.00. Don't worry about supper. I'll fix something when I get back.

Denis

Ps. Could you ring Sam and tell him I'll help him with the letter another evening.
Thanks

3. Write a note to someone you know well:

– tell him/her you are going out somewhere (say where and why)
– say when you think you'll be back
– ask him/her to do something for you.

Start like this:

I've just remembered I've got to/a . . .
I've just been asked to . . .
. . . has just phoned to say/ask . . .
I'm afraid I've got to . . .

Dr James' story

Use the following key words to talk about what has happened so far:

Dr James/phone call/patient ill/Aldhurst Farm, near Capel/as soon as possible/note for wife/drove off

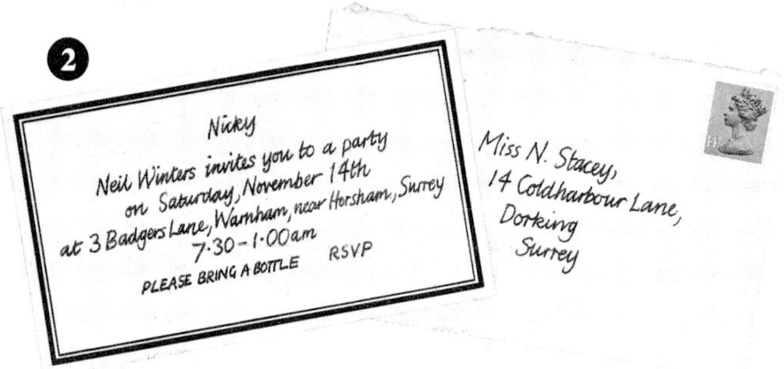
Nicky
Neil Winters invites you to a party
on Saturday, November 14th
at 3 Badgers Lane, Warnham, near Horsham, Surrey
7·30 – 1·00am
RSVP
PLEASE BRING A BOTTLE

Miss N. Stacey,
14 Coldharbour Lane,
Dorking
Surrey

Nicky Stacey is 18. She lives at home with her parents, and works for an estate agent in Dorking. Her boyfriend, Dale, lives in Ockley, near Capel.

Check

What do you know about Nicky?
What is she going to do on Saturday, 14th November?

1. Fill in the missing verbs in the following written invitation. Choose the right form of the verbs:

meet, look, have, do, be, hear, think, make, see, write, wonder, can.

Dear Sarah,

I apologise for not ..... earlier but I've ..... very busy at work. I was ..... the other day that it ..... ages since we last .....

I don't know if you ..... free but I'm ..... a small party on Saturday, 10th January, with just a few of our friends, and I was ..... if you ..... possibly come. It would be such fun to ..... you again. Do try and ..... it.

..... forward to ..... from you.

Much love,
Joannie

2. Writing

Now write a similar letter to a good friend of yours whom you have not seen or heard from for some time. Invite your friend to a lunch party (give date) to which you have invited your parents, a few neighbours, and some friends.

3.

Nicky asks her mother if she can borrow the car to go to the party.

NICKY: Mum, do you think I could borrow the car this evening? Dale and I have been invited to a party and Dale's bike isn't working.

MUM: Yes, I suppose so. It's safer than that motorbike of his, anyway. But for goodness sake, drive carefully. It's been raining all day and the roads are bound to be very wet and slippery.

NICKY: Yes, I will. Thanks, Mum.

Now ask your partner if you can borrow:

- a piece of clothing (scarf, jacket, sweater)
- his/her bicycle
- a record of his/hers.

Give a reason for borrowing the article each time.

4. Listening

Nicky's boyfriend, Dale, has also been invited to the party. Nicky telephones him to arrange where to meet him. Listen to their conversation and find on the map on page 30 where Nicky is going to pick up Dale. Then complete these sentences:

Dale told Nicky that he couldn't . . .
Nicky told Dale that she could . . .
Dale told Nicky to meet . . . at . . .
He told Nicky not to . . . because . . .

Nicky and Dale's story

Use the following key words to talk about what has happened so far:

Nicky/party in Horsham/boyfriend's motorbike not working/asked mother/family car/telephoned Dale/meet (where? when?)/drove off.

Name: Heather Innes
Age: 35
Occupation: Sports journalist

HEATHER INNES

Winter Sports coverage

Travel details

November 14th

Heathrow Airport:	Report 21.00
Flight BA257:	Depart 22.00
Munich Airport:	Arrive 23.30

Dear Jock,

I've just learnt that I have to go to Innsbruck on Saturday, 14th November, to cover the winter sports. I don't expect I'll be back before Wednesday so I'm afraid I won't be able to come to the meeting on Tuesday. I'm very sorry I couldn't let you know earlier. I'll do the report when I get back.

Yours,

Heather

Check

What do you know about Heather?
What is she going to do on Saturday evening, November 14th? Why?

1. Writing

Now write a similar informal letter to your teacher. Explain that you have to go away for a few weeks and therefore won't be able to come to classes. Say when you expect to be back. Say you will catch up with the work when you get back.

2. Listening

Heather asks a friend of hers, Peter, to go with her to the airport so that she won't have to leave her car. Listen to their conversation as they leave, and answer these questions:

Who is going to drive? Why?
Which route are they going to take to London Heathrow Airport?

Check

What are the weather conditions like?
Why isn't the car in perfect condition?

Heather's story

Use the following key words to talk about what has happened so far:

Heather Innes/sports journalist/Innsbruck/Heathrow Airport/Peter/A24/drove off/windscreen wipers.

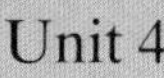

4

ROCK UNLIMITED

... and winner of the Young Talent Award, is a group from Horsham in Surrey called Rock Unlimited. Lead singer and song writer, Dave Starr, says they are about to release their first album with Fantasy Records called *Stretching Ahead*.

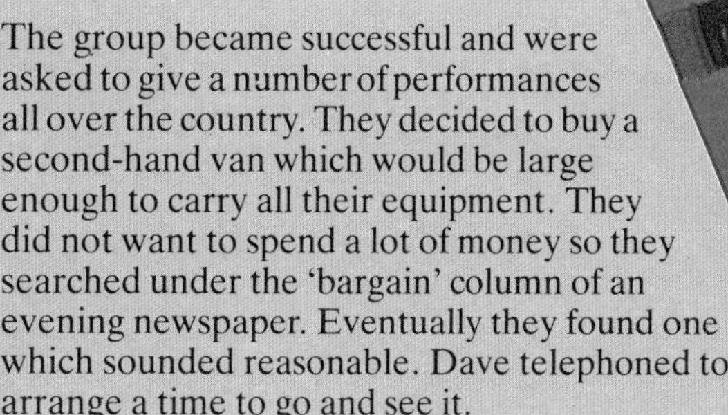

The group became successful and were asked to give a number of performances all over the country. They decided to buy a second-hand van which would be large enough to carry all their equipment. They did not want to spend a lot of money so they searched under the 'bargain' column of an evening newspaper. Eventually they found one which sounded reasonable. Dave telephoned to arrange a time to go and see it.

> The group became successful and were asked to give a number of performances . . .
> or
> *Having become* successful, the group were asked to give a number of performances . . .

1. Join the following sentences in the same way:

They decided to buy . . ./they searched in a newspaper . . .
They searched in a newspaper . . ./they eventually found one.
They found one which . . ./Dave telephoned to . . .

2. Listening

Listen to Dave's conversation and identify the correct advertisement for the van from the selection on the right. Then fill in Dave's part of the conversation.

AVENGER 1972 MoT, tax, radio, extras. £450. 556 0277.

VANDEN PLAS PRINCESS 1300. G reg, new clutch, vgc. £495 ono. 580 4602 (day).

HILLMAN MINX, '61, year's MoT, long tax, 2 owners, 48,000 miles, immac. £250. 321 1856.

MORRIS 1000 VAN. 1970, tax, tested. £200 ono. 946 0275.

TRANSIT VAN, '73, taxed, MoT, low mileage. £475. 01-794 5922 after 6p.m.

CHRYSLER 180. K reg, blue, very good body, numerous spares. £395. 606 2159.

WOMAN: 794 5922
DAVE: Oh, hello. I'm . . .
WOMAN: Yes, it is.
DAVE: . . . .
WOMAN: Yes, sure. It's had one or two knocks but it's pretty sound.
DAVE: . . . .
WOMAN: £475. Yes, that's right.
DAVE: . . . .
WOMAN: Yes, OK. When were you thinking of coming?
DAVE: . . . .
WOMAN: Any time between 4 and 8 this evening.
DAVE: . . . .
WOMAN: Yes, it's 70 South Hill Park . . .

5

Now look at the following advertisements. In pairs, act out the telephone conversations in which you arrange to go and see (i) the typewriter and (ii) the house. Use the language you have learnt from Dave's conversation

BRIGHTON, charming second-floor flat, in Regency terrace with sea views, lounge, double bedroom, large kitchen, luxury bathroom with shower, gas central heating. Carpets included. £21,000 ono. Bexhill (0424) 224475 (before 5pm.).

RENT a fridge from 50p per week – 845 2618 (Days). U13059.

PORTABLE typewriters, a selection of reconditioned machines from £16. On offer for one month only or while stocks last. Hurry hurry – Regent Typewriters. 504 8934. F69048.

RECORDS, singles, LPs, 12in. a big varied collection. £275 ono – Phone Steve 719 8238. S05243

Saturday

ROCK ☆ ☆ ☆

ROCK UNLIMITED Half Moon, Putney, Putney Bridge

District Line. 9.00pm £3.

Check

What do you know about the group, Rock Unlimited?

Where are they going on Saturday, 14th November? Why?

Use the advertisement above to fill in the missing parts of this conversation. Jake is inviting Mac to come with him to the Half Moon for the evening.

JAKE: What are you doing on ....?

MAC: ....

JAKE: Well, why ....?

MAC: ....

JAKE: Oh, go on! I've heard they're a good group.

MAC: ....

JAKE: It's not far from Putney Bridge station on the District Line.

MAC: ....

JAKE: It says nine o'clock in *Time Out* but let's meet a bit earlier, at about 8.30.

MAC: ....

JAKE: Yes, I'm afraid so. £3.

MAC: ....

JAKE: I can lend you some if you're a bit short of money. Anyway, think about it and give me a ring later.

Now use this advertisement to act out a similar conversation.

Bands, Food, Drink, Skate Hire, Tuition, Amusements. 124 Shepherds Bush Road, London W6. 01-608 2469

Monday-Closed

Tuesday
2-6pm Skating £1.50 Hire 50p
8pm TUITION AND PRACTICE
£2.00 incl. hire of skates

Wednesday
2-6pm Skating £1.50 Hire 50p
8pm-12.30 CHEAP SKATES NIGHT
£1.50 Hire £1.00

Thursday
2-6pm Skating £1.50 Hire 50p
8pm-12.30 OPEN NIGHT
£2.50 Hire £1.00

Friday
2-6pm Skating £1.50 Hire 50p
8pm-12.30 OPEN NIGHT
£2.50 Hire £1.00

Saturday
Children and Adults 10.30am-12.30
£1.00 Tuition 50p Hire 50p
2-6pm General Skating £1.50 Hire 50p
8pm-12.30 OPEN NIGHT
£2.50 Hire £1.00

Sunday
Children and Adults 10.30am-12.30
£1.00 Tuition 50p Hire 50p
2-6pm General Skating £1.50 Hire 50p
8.00pm-12.30 OPEN NIGHT
£2.50 Hire £1.00

We plan to have live bands, shows, demos, competitions, team games etc. For participation & details contact us!!

The group's story

Use these key words to talk about what has happened so far.

Rock Unlimited/talent award/performances/second-hand van/Putney/Saturday, 14th November/drove off/7.45 pm.

6

Police seek hit-and-run driver on A24

Dorking girl seriously injured

DAILY NEWS REPORTER

Dorking police are still looking for the driver of a Ford Transit van which failed to stop after causing an accident on the A24 between Beare Green and Capel. The accident involved three other cars, a Cortina, an Austin Princess and an MGB.

The driver of the Cortina, 18-year-old Nicola Stacey from Dorking, was taken to hospital for an emergency operation to save her eyesight.

Dr James, driver of the Austin Princess, was on his way to see a patient in Capel. Said Dr James, 'I was keeping my distance behind the Cortina when I saw a van coming very fast in the opposite direction on the wrong side of the road. The Cortina braked and swerved to avoid it, but the van must have hit its front wing because it overturned and landed in the ditch.'

Dr James said he called an ambulance and Miss Stacey was taken to Dorking General Hospital for emergency treatment. No-one else was hurt.

Miss Heather Innes, driver of the MGB, said, 'When I saw the van overtake me and the other car coming, I swerved to the left to get out of the way. I ran into the hedge but luckily we didn't hurt ourselves. Miss Innes and her companion, Mr Peter Walford, were on their way to Heathrow Airport. Said Miss Innes. 'The worst part of it was that I missed my plane.'

1. Find the place where the accident occurred on the map on page 30.

2. Make a sketch map showing the position of the four cars at the moment of the accident.

3. Match the two halves of the sentences to make true statements about the accident, like this: A–3.

A The van caused an accident
B The Cortina swerved to avoid the van
C The doctor looked at the condition of the girl
D Heather Innes saw the van hit the other car
E Heather Innes stopped to act as a witness at the scene of the accident

1 and so she swerved to get out of the way.
2 and he immediately called for an ambulance.
3 and then drove on without stopping.
4 and so missed her plane from Heathrow Airport.
5 and then overturned and landed in a ditch.

Then rewrite the sentences, joining the two halves with 'having'+past participle, **like this:**
(A–3) Having caused an accident, the van drove on without stopping.

4. Imagine you are a police officer. You have found the Transit van and you are interviewing the driver, Dave Starr. With a partner, ask and answer these questions:

Where were you going?
How fast were you driving?
Why did you overtake?
Didn't you see the Cortina coming?

Ask any other questions that you think are important.

5. In pairs act out the telephone conversations between:

- Nicky's boyfriend, Dale, and her parents when she doesn't arrive at Capel to pick him up.
- a nurse at Dorking Hospital and Nicky's parents.

6. Write out one of the drivers' statements to the police in full. Start like this:

I was on my way to ....

Oral exercises

1. Expressing expectation

Alison is going abroad to work. Her friend, Luke, is asking her what she feels about it.

So you're going to live in New York, are you?
Yes, I'm quite looking forward to living there, actually.

1. So you're going to live in New York, are you?
2. And you've got a job at the Trade Centre, I hear?
3. You'll meet that Russian woman, you know, the Economic Adviser.
4. Doesn't your sister live somewhere near New York, too?
5. Well, it'll be nice to leave England at this time of year.

2. Forecasting time (Open exercise)

You're off to the cinema, are you?
Yes, I don't expect I'll be back before eleven.

1. football match
2. matinée at the theatre
3. discotheque
4. dentist appointment
5. cocktail party

3. Asking permission to borrow things

Do you think I could borrow your car?
Yes, as long as I can have it back tomorrow.

Do you think you could lend me your car?
Yes, as long as I can have it back tomorrow.

1. road map
2. dictionary
3. scarf
4. umbrella
5. £1
6. bike

4. Breaking arrangements and appointments

You can't come to next Tuesday's class. Telephone your teacher.

TEACHER: Hello, Peter Hallas here.
STUDENT: *Oh, hello. This is Brian Hunter here. I'm just phoning to say that I'm afraid I won't be able to come to class next Tuesday.*

1. Telephone your friend. You can't come to her party on Saturday.
2. Telephone the dentist. You can't keep your appointment on Wednesday at four.
3. Telephone the college. You can't come to the students' meeting on Friday afternoon.
4. Telephone the hairdresser. You can't keep your appointment on Friday morning at eleven.

5. Making predictions

Tom is packing to go for a weekend in the country. He is asking advice about things to take.

Shall I pack my Wellington boots?
Yes, it's bound to be wet

Choose between 'wet', and 'cold'.
Tom asks about the following:

1. thick sweater
2. a pack of cards
3. some extra blankets
4. gloves
5. umbrella

Unit 4 Study focus

Interaction

FUNCTION	STRUCTURE
1. Giving and following directions	prepositional phrases: position and motion
2. Forecasting times	'I (don't) expect' + 'will'
3. Narrating events	past simple and continuous time markers
4. Making polite requests	'Do you think I could borrow/lend . . .'
5. Predicting	'bound to' + infinitive
6. Breaking arrangements	'I'm afraid I won't be able to . . .'

ADDITIONAL STRUCTURES
past participle phrases:
'having searched . . . they found . . .'

Vocabulary
Weather conditions
Cars
Driving

Writing skills
1. Sentence building from key words: narrative
2. Guided paragraphs: narrative
3. Guided informal letter of invitation
4. Polite informal letter: breaking arrangements with explanation
5. Composition about an accident seen or experienced: descriptive and narrative

Unit 5 Consolidation

1

Look at the picture of the umbrella and read the description.

a red collapsible umbrella with a black handle and strap

Now look at the rest of the pictures. These are some objects which have been handed in to a police station. Write the policeman's description of each item.

Date	Item No.	Description	Where found	Claimed
23-5-82	1	A green ladies' bicycle with a basket at the front	Station yard	
"	2		Hatton Crescent	
"	3		Clevedon Hotel	
"	4		Ladies room	
"	5		No. 65 bus	

2 Listening

Listen to a Crime Prevention Officer talking about burglars. Note what he says about:
(i) the character of a burglar (ii) the time of most burglaries (iii) the way a burglar needs to operate (iv) what would deter a burglar.

FOOTBALL FANS RUN RIOT

BY DAVID JAMES

A crowd of disappointed football fans caused thousands of pounds worth of damage in Sheffield after the defeat of their team on Saturday afternoon by Manchester United . . .

What do you think the fans did to the following:

a public telephone box?
some bus seats?
a shop window?
a parked car?
a launderette?
an automatic vending machine?

1. Now report the incidents as if you were present at the scene, like this:

'Look! The telephone has been torn out of that public telephone box!'

Now finish writing the article. Start like this:
'. . . Among other things, a telephone was torn out of a . . .'

2. Make negatives of the following adjectives, using a prefix: in . . . un . . . im . . . dis . . .
or a suffix: . . .less

patient	tolerant	attractive
sensitive	honest	intelligent
adventurous	humorous	
tactful	sincere	

Read the following notes which an employer made after interviewing several candidates for a job. The employer didn't think any of the people were suitable. Choose the most suitable adjective from the list you made in Exercise 2.

5 Listening

Jane is explaining to her mother why she does not like her history teacher, Mr Taylor. What explanations does she give for these qualities in Mr Taylor?

boring:
quick tempered:
vain:
conceited:
cruel:

❻ Letter writing

Imagine you are giving instructions for writing this letter. Complete the following sentences using the key words provided, like this:

Why/writing: You should say why you are writing the letter.

How to write the letter:

You should say:
1. Why/writing
2. What/lost
3. When/lost
4. Where/think lost
5. What/like
6. How/reached

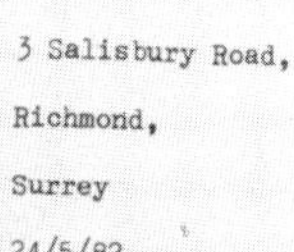

3 Salisbury Road,
Richmond,
Surrey
24/5/82

The Manager,
Cleveland Hotel,
Royston

Dear Sir,

I am writing to ask if you have found a ladies' watch in the cloakroom of your hotel.

My husband and I had lunch at your hotel on Monday and I remember taking the watch off in the ladies' cloakroom to wash my hands. I think I must have left it beside the wash basin. It is a small, gold Ingersoll watch with a white leather strap.

If anybody has found it, perhaps you could telephone me on 940 7564 or write and let me know.

Yours faithfully,

Jean Booker

Jean Booker

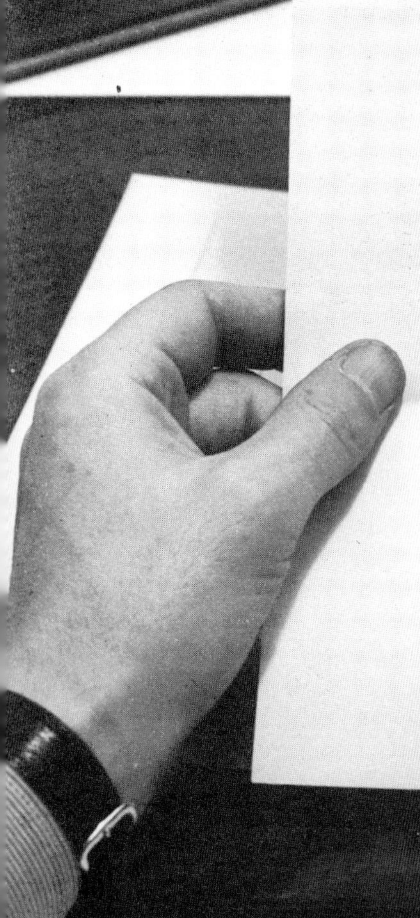

Layout

Some points to remember:

1. Write *your address only* (not your name) at the top right hand of the letter.
2. Write the date underneath your address. Here are some ways of writing the date:
   November 7th, 1982   7th November, 1982   7/11/82
3. Write the name or title, and address of the addressee (the person to whom you are writing) above
   'Dear . . .'
4. If you know the name of the addressee, start your letter
   'Dear Mr/Mrs/Ms . . .' and end it 'Yours sincerely'. If you do not know the name of the addressee but only his/her title (e.g. The Secretary, The Manager etc.), start 'Dear Sir/Madam' and end it 'Yours faithfully'.
5. Sign your name, and then print it underneath your signature so that it can easily be read.
6. Use either *block* or *indented* style for your own address but do not mix the two. Use the block only for the addressee on the letter.

Block	*Indented*
3, Salisbury Road,	3, Salisbury Road
Richmond,	Richmond,
Surrey.	Surrey.

Study the following layout of a formal letter and see how many things wrong you can find. There are at least five.

Write the letter out again in your notebooks in the correct way.

```
The Manager                                  Catherine Juillet
The Grand Hotel                               32 Mitcham Way
Marine Parade                                    Selsdon
Brighton                                          Surrey
                                            the 4th of june
                    Dear Manager,
I would like to book a room at your hotel for three nights
from August 1st to August 4th.
I look forward to hearing from you.
Yours sincerely,
Catherine Juillet
```

Content

A formal letter may contain four parts:

PART 1 *Make a point of reference* for the addressee, like this:
'With reference to your letter. . .'

PART 2 *State the purpose* of your letter.

PART 3 *Give information* that may be relevant or useful.

PART 4 *Close the letter* by mentioning what action you are expecting the addressee to make, e.g. write, telephone, send something.

1. Here are some common phrases taken from formal letters. Say which part you think they belong to:

1. I look forward to hearing from you.
2. I saw your advertisement in *The New Standard* of November 14th.
3. You may remember meeting me at . . .
4. As far as I remember, the wallet contained . . .
5. I was wondering if you could send me some details . . .
6. If you find it, perhaps you could phone me on 997 8657
7. I have had several years' experience as a . . .
8. I would be very grateful if you could send me some . . .

2. Read the letter to the Manager of the Cleveland Hotel and notice how the paragraphs are divided.

Imagine that you have lost either a **bracelet, a watch** or **an address book at the Cleveland Hotel. Write a similar letter to the manager of the hotel.**

In the first paragraph, state the *purpose* of your letter.

In the second paragraph, say:
– when you lost the object
– where and how you lost it
– what it looks like.

In the third paragraph, tell the manager how to contact you.

7

Somerset Maugham painted by Graham Sutherland

I never knew his name. He did not offer to tell me and I did not like to ask it. I will call him Jean Charvin.

I met him on my first visit to the camp with the commandant. We were walking through a courtyard round which were cells, not punishment cells, but individual cells which are given to well-behaved prisoners who ask for them. They are sought after by those to whom the promiscuity of the dormitories is odious. Most of them were empty, for their occupants were engaged in their various employments. Jean Charvin was at work in his cell, writing at a small table, and the door was open. The commandant called him and he came out. I looked into the cell. It contained a fixed hammock, with a dingy mosquito-net; by the side of this was a small table on which were his bits and pieces, a shaving-mop and a razor, a hairbrush and two or three battered books. On the walls were photographs of persons of respectable appearance and illustrations from picture papers. He had been sitting on his bed to write and the table on which he had been writing was covered with papers. They looked like accounts. He was a handsome man, tall, erect, and lean, with flashing dark eyes and clean-cut, strong features. The first thing I noticed about him was that he had a fine head of long, naturally-waving dark brown hair. This at once made him look different from the rest of the prisoners, whose hair is close-cropped, but cropped so badly, in ridges, that it gives them a sinister look. The commandant spoke to him of some official business, and then as we were leaving, added in a friendly way:

'I see your hair is growing well.'

Jean Charvin reddened and smiled. His smile was boyish and engaging.

'It'll be some time yet before I get it right again.'

The commandant dismissed him and we went on.

'He's a very decent fellow,' he said. 'He's in the accountant's department, and he's had leave to let his hair grow. He's delighted.'

'What is he here for?' I asked.

'He killed his wife. But he's only got six years. He's clever and a good worker. He'll do well. He comes from a very decent family and he's had an excellent education.'

I thought no more of Jean Charvin, but by chance I met him next day on the road. He was coming towards me. He carried a black dispatch-case under his arm, and except for the pink and white stripes of his uniform and the ugly round straw hat that concealed his handsome head of hair, you might have taken him for a young lawyer on his way to court. He walked with a long, leisurely stride, and he had an easy, you might almost say a gallant, bearing. He recognised me, and taking off his hat bade me good morning. I stopped, and for something to say asked him where he was going. He told me he was taking some papers from the governor's office to the bank. There was a pleasing frankness in his face, and his eyes, his really beautiful eyes, shone with goodwill. I supposed that the vigour of his youth was such that it made life, notwithstanding his position and his surroundings, more than tolerable, even pleasant. You would have said that here was a young man without a care in the world.

From *A Man with a Conscience*, a short story by Somerset Maugham

1. Summarise the official details of Jean Charvin's case in this form:

Name	*Jean Charvin*
Offence	
Sentence	
Appearance	
Background	
Prison occupation	
General behaviour	

2. How does the author describe Jean Charvin's appearance and personality? List the words and phrases he uses, like this:

handsome

Which of the words and phrases in your list show the author's own attitude to Jean Charvin? Is the attitude positive or negative? For example:

handsome: positive

3. Find the following words from the text in your dictionary. Write the correct definitions of the base forms.

dormitories (line 8): dormitory – a large room . . .

odious (line 9)
battered (line 17)
lean (line 23)
cropped (line 28)
ridges (line 29)
bade (line 54)
vigour (line 60)

4. Look at line 7.

'Them' refers to 'cells' in line 5.

What do the following pronouns refer to? Give the exact word or phrase and the line number.

line 7 they
line 8 those
line 9 their
line 26 this
line 29 it
line 29 them
line 35 it
line 60 it

5. At several points in the text, the author indicates that Jean Charvin is considered trustworthy. List these indications.

8 A friendly argument

Juliet wants to go abroad for a holiday but Steve wants to stay at home, in Britain. Read their conversation and note down the points for and against both types of holiday. First, here are some useful phrases from the conversation.

INTRODUCING POINTS 'FOR'	INTRODUCING POINTS 'AGAINST'	LINKING TWO POINTS 'FOR' or 'AGAINST'
Think of . . . The best thing about . . . is . . .	Yes, but . . . But look, . . . I'm sorry, I just don't . . . Even so, . . . Nevertheless, . . .	And another thing, . . . Anyway, . . . And what's more, . . .

Use the ideas and the language on this page to write a short dialogue between two friends who are planning a holiday. The two friends could be discussing the points for and against two of the following:

- having a holiday with the whole family.
- a camping holiday.
- a working holiday.
- a holiday at an English language school.

JULIET: Why don't we go abroad for a change? Where I'd like to go is France, Spain, or Italy even.

STEVE: Mm. I'm not all that keen really. I'd rather stay at home.

JULIET: Oh, come on, Steve. Think of the sun!

STEVE: Yes, but think of the cost! Going abroad is very expensive.

JULIET: Oh, it isn't Steve. Not these days.

STEVE: Of course it is, Juliet. The best thing about having a holiday here in Britain is that it's cheaper. And another thing, the travelling would be easier. No boats, planes or anything.

JULIET: Even so, we've been to most of the interesting places in Britain already. What's the point in seeing them again? Anyway, we can travel round Britain whenever we like. There's no point in wasting our summer holiday here.

STEVE: Mm, I suppose you're right. Nevertheless, what I can't stand is all the bother with foreign currency, changing money and all that when we go abroad. I hate all that. And it's so confusing.

JULIET: Oh, don't be silly, Steve.

STEVE: And what's more, I can't speak any of the languages – you know that. It's all right for you. You can speak foreign languages.

JULIET: Exactly. You see, what I'd really like to do is practise my French and Spanish. It would help me a lot at work.

STEVE: Mm, but that's no use to me.

JULIET: But just think of the new places we'd see, the people we'd meet!

STEVE: But look, if we stayed here, we wouldn't have to plan very much.

JULIET: I'm sorry, Steve. No. I just don't fancy another cold English summer.

A HOLIDAY ABROAD	
Points for (advantages)	Points against (disadvantages)
1	1
2	2
3	3

A HOLIDAY AT HOME	
Points for (advantages)	Points against (disadvantages)
1	1
2	2
3	3

Writing tasks

1. *A note*
   Write a note to a friend or relative telling him/her that you have just gone to the library. Say when you expect to be back. Ask him/her to take any messages if anyone telephones while you are out.

2. *An informal letter*
   Write a letter to a friend or relative. Apologise for not writing before. Explain what you have been doing recently. Invite him/her to come and stay for the weekend (name a day). Ask him/her to let you know if it is possible.

3. *A formal letter*
   Write a letter of polite complaint to the manager of the hotel where you stayed for your summer holiday. Although you paid your bill on leaving the hotel, the manager has sent you another one for the same amount, demanding immediate payment.

4. *A list*
   Make a list of items (clothes, accessories, toilet articles etc.) that you would pack for a week's holiday in the south of Spain in August.

5. *A holiday advertisement*
   Write an attractive advertisement for a holiday in a famous tourist resort in your country.

6. *A notice*
   You have lost your cat. Write a notice to put into the local newsagent's window.

7. *A 'For Sale' advertisement*
   You are selling your car/bicycle/motorbike. Write an advertisement suitable for a newspaper. Write no more than 25 words.

8. *A conversation*
   It is Saturday afternoon. Your brother wants to go to a football match. Try to persuade him to do something else instead. Write in dialogue form, giving only the name of each speaker, followed by the actual words spoken.

...ll,
I suddenly realised that my books were overdue so I've just popped out to the librar... I won't be long. Back about 3. I'm expecti... a couple of phone calls this afternoon. Co... you kindly take any messages? Oh, and i... Steve calls tell him the card was lovel... that I'll see him as we arranged on Sunday.

Kate

35, Cliff Road,
Folkestone,
Kent

Tuesday, May 10th

Dear Tom,

Many thanks for your postcard from Alaska. What were you doing there by the way? I am sorry I haven't written to you recently, but I've been travelling too. I had to go out to Saudi Arabia to sort out a problem that occurred in one of our schools. I was out there for two months so that explains why you haven't heard from me.

Anyway, I wonder if you, Annie and the children would like to come down and spend the Bank Holiday weekend with us. You could drive down on the Thursday evening when the traffic isn't so bad and stay until the following Tuesday. We've got plenty of spare beds and I am sure the children would enjoy a few days by the sea.

We would really like to see you all and hear all your news, so do try to make it. Let me know ...

...er.
...nie and the kids.
...ours,
Norman

---

24 Eaton Road,
Harrow,
Middx.

September 16th 19...

The Manager,
Bellevue Hotel,
Poole, Dorset

Dear Sir,

Thank you for your letter of September 1... Unfortunately there seems to be some mis... understanding over the payment of our bi...

My family and I stayed at your hotel between August 9th and August 23rd this year. On leaving the hotel, I paid the bill as requested. Yesterday morning I received a letter from you implying that I had not yet settled the bill. In reply, I enclose ... receipt which your receptionist gave m... the time and hope that it will help you clear the matter up as soon as possible.

I look forward to hearing from you.

Yours faithfully,

A. R. Sallows

A. R. Sallows

It's always festival time in Munich

Munich is Germany's most festive city. Summer is one big festival season with concerts and the famous Opera Festival. In the autumn there is the Oktoberfest, a lively beer festival. Later there is Munich's favourite Christmas market. Munich has something for everybody at any time.

Famous museums, parks, fashionable shopping centres, beergardens, the nightlife of Schwabing's artists' quarter ...... And just outside is the beautiful Bavarian countryside. Take a festive holiday in Munich. Post the coupon below for full details.

HOLIDAY THINGS

TO BUY
sandals
sun tan cream
shampoo and conditioner
nice big beach towel
oil remover
insect repellent
don't forget BANK
and travellers' cheques
spare film
sun specs
new hold-all
P.S. Go to library for guidebook to Southern Spain.

TO TAKE TO CLEANERS
silk dress
blouses
white trousers
pick up raincoat

LOST

BEAUTIFUL MARMALADE CAT WITH WHITE PAWS. ANSWERS TO THE NAME OF 'BUGSIE'. LOST SOMETIME ON SUNDAY MARCH 10TH. IF FOUND, PLEASE RING 696 993 (AFTER 6 pm PLEASE) OR RETURN TO: HUDSON, FLAT 2, 44 INGLIS AVENUE, W5

FOLDAWAY RALEIGH BIKE
Almost new with all accessories – lights etc. In excellent working condition. Green and gold.
ONLY £50 Phone Terry — 236 8950

BROTHER: Do you want to come to the football match?
YOU: What now?
BROTHER: Yes. Spurs versus Chelsea.
YOU: Oh no, not football. You know I don't enjoy it that much. Can't we go to the cinema instead?
BROTHER: Look, we can go to the cinema any time. Besides, it's too expensive.
YOU: But I don't like football! For one thing, it's cold standing out in the drizzle, and another thing, they never score a goal when I go. It's deathly boring.
BROTHER: Come on! Don't be silly! They say it's going to be the match of the season.
YOU: Even so, I really would prefer the cinema. They're showing 'Superman II' at the local and you know how much you've been looking forward to seeing that.
BROTHER: Mmm. Well, let's toss a coin. Heads we go to the match and tails we go to the cinema. How about that?

Unit 6 A question of taste

Before you start:

What sort of paintings, films, plays and music do you like?
Do you ever read reviews of films or plays in newspapers or magazines?
Will this decide whether you go to see the film or play?

1

Is this the most beautiful painting in the world? A lot of people think so. It is Leonardo da Vinci's *La Giaconda,* also known as the *Mona Lisa*. This most famous of all portraits, painted around 1503, can be seen in the Louvre Museum, Paris.

They say that each time you look at her, you see something different . . .

Do you like *La Giaconda?* If so, why? If not, why not?
Why do you think that this painting is so famous and well liked? Is the secret – in her hands? – in her eyes? – in her smile?

2 [cassette]

Gerry and Judy are visiting a famous art gallery and they have a difference of opinion. Read the dialogue in pairs.

GERRY: A portrait? Is that a portrait?!
JUDY: Yes. I like it. I think it's great, don't you?
GERRY: No, it's too modern for my taste. That sort of thing doesn't appeal to me. It doesn't even look like a person.
JUDY: But that's how the artist saw the person. He saw the inner person, not the surface.
GERRY: It's all a load of rubbish. Anyway, who is the artist?
JUDY: Picasso, of course!
GERRY: Oh, is it? Well, I'm sorry. It does nothing for me. I don't know what you see in it. Come on, let's go on into the next room . . . Ah, now *this* is more to my taste. This is the sort of thing *I* really like!

'Seated Woman' by Picasso

1. Make a list of the different ways of expressing taste, like this:

LIKES
I like it.
I think it's great.
. . . .

DISLIKES
It's too modern for my taste.
. . . .

2. Now look at the two paintings below. Discuss in pairs or groups whether they appeal to you or not. Try to use some of the expressions from the dialogue in the first column.

'The Hay Wain' by Constable

'Apparition of face and fruit dish on a beach' by Dali

Two people were asked to write a description of a painting which they liked very much.

One of my favourite paintings is a watercolour called *Sailing Village in Winter.* It is painted by an unknown local artist.

The picture shows the waterfront at low-tide. A few sailing boats are moored just off the mud bank and a few houses nestle at the water's edge.

I particularly like the artist's use of colour. The whitish-grey clouds scurrying across the sky and the silvery-grey sea are relieved only by the brown of the mud bank and the red brick roofs of the houses.

The painting appeals to me because it is peaceful and realistic. You can almost hear the gulls calling, you can almost smell the sea and taste the salt on your lips and hair. When I look at the picture, I feel I am there.

A picture I have always liked is a small charcoal sketch by an artist called Mulready Stone. It doesn't have a name but it is a sketch of a street scene in Spain. A woman, dressed in peasant clothes, is leaning against a dark archway selling apples. The apples are heaped in a basket by her feet. One of the reasons I like the sketch is the artist's attention to detail: the expression in the woman's eyes, the fold of her dress and the odd apple lying in the gutter. His use of light and shade is also effective.

In my opinion it is a very moving and beautiful sketch. It is also, in some ways, rather exciting and exotic. I can almost smell the foreign city and hear the foreign cries in my ears. It is a picture I can look at again and again, and always find something different in it.

1. In which order do both the writers mention the following?

the subject of the painting
the artist's skills
the effect of the painting on the writer
the type of painting
the writer's opinion of the painting
the title of the painting
the name of the artist.

2. Under each heading note down how each point is introduced, and any special vocabulary used. Here is an example:

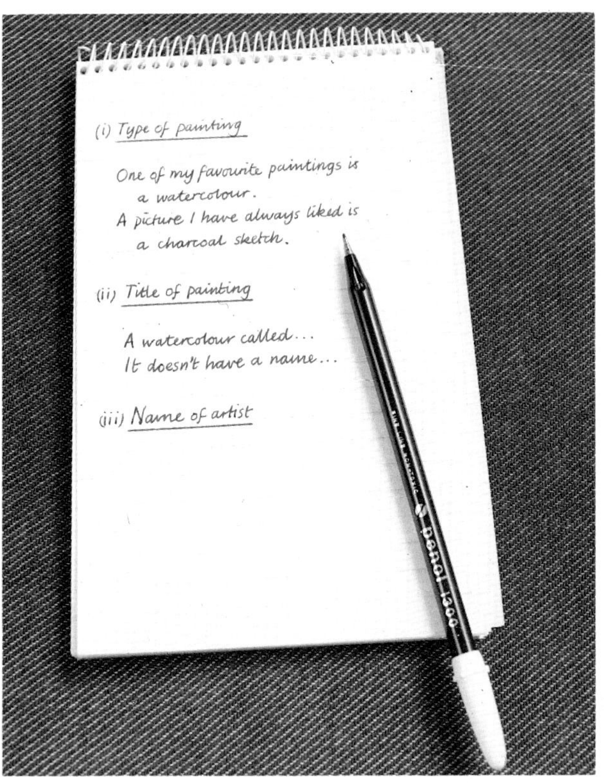

3. Describe and discuss some of the paintings on the previous pages.

Think of a painting that you like — perhaps it is in your house or in your school, or at an art gallery – and write a few paragraphs saying what it is like and why you like it. Use the paragraphs on the left to help you.

❹ Critical reviews

Most British newspapers and magazines have regular reviews of films, books, plays, concerts and so on. Look at these quotations from some reviews and complete the chart.

QUOTATIONS	REFERENCE To which does it principally refer: book, film, ballet, concert, play?	REACTION Favourable, unfavourable or neutral?
1. but the dancing was stiff and awkward		
2. the second movement was too slow		
3. each chapter deals with a different aspect		
4. the acting in the first scene was superb		
5. the desert scenes were all shot on location		
6. the brilliant soloist for last night's concerto was . . .		
7. the stage is extended out into the audience		
8. and the text is supported by beautiful illustrations		
9. last night's symphony was conducted by . . .		
10. the flashback sequences were confusing and contrived		
11. and for this production there is a new choreographer		
12. the narrative in the last pages moves clumsily towards its climax		
13. the grace and strength of the Russian pair was evident in the magnificent pas de deux		
14. . . .for a supreme moment of horror, the close-up of the crawling ants . . .		
15. the production was notable for the incomprehension with which the lines were delivered		

Word study

(i) Group all the words to do with ballet, film and so on, like this:

BALLET	FILM	PLAY
dancing	shot	
choreographer		

(ii) Group all the words or expressions which give a favourable or an unfavourable meaning, like this:

FAVOURABLE	UNFAVOURABLE
superb	stiff
	awkward

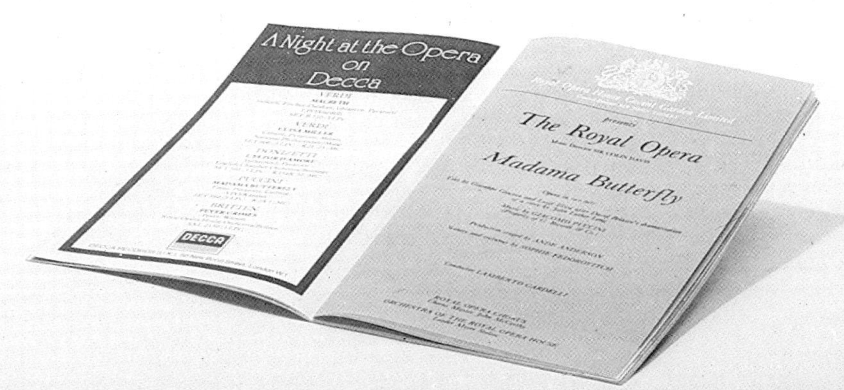

5

1. Read and classify the following reviews under these headings:

TYPE (e.g. film, play, book)	TITLE & AUTHOR OR DIRECTOR /PRODUCER	MAIN ACTORS & ACTRESSES	GENERAL OPINION (e.g. favourable/ unfavourable
Example: Play	*Macbeth* by William Shakespeare	Peter O'Toole	unfavourable

In September 1980, the famous actor, Peter O'Toole, both produced and played the leading role in Shakespeare's *Macbeth*. The production received the worst reviews that anyone could remember. The critics' reactions made front-page news in all the newspapers.

Macbeth: don't trust those reviews

Peter O'Toole's *Macbeth* opened this week to *titters* from the audience and the worst reviews of the year.

Don't trust those reviews. The spectacle is far worse than has hitherto been made out, a milestone in the history of *coarse* acting.

The production was notable for the *incomprehension* with which lines were delivered and for the most wild moments of 'interpretation.'

As to Mr O'Toole's performance, it was *deranged*. 'I have,' says Macbeth, 'a strange infirmity which is nothing to those that know me.' At first, I thought that this must be a portrayal of drunkenness.

Xanadu

Critical comment: A ragbag collection of pop singles staged as production numbers, love scenes, rollerskating capers, etc., linked by a pretentiously silly and sentimental story, too long in the telling. The co-starring of Gene Kelly is a sorry sight for his long-time fans, and the related pseudo-nostalgia of Forties type big-band music is flopperoo time, only partially relieved by the stylised routines of the ensemble dancers. The special effects are flashy and crude, and the colour of the print under review made the principals look weatherbeaten and sun-dried. The quality of the sound seemed equally rough.

Very young fans of Oliva Newton-John will doubtless enjoy *Xanadu* well enough, though Zeus only knows what they'll make of all the gobbledegook about the Muses, Kubla Khan and Glenn Miller.

David Lynch's *The Elephant Man* (ABC Shaftesbury Avenue AA) opens with a strangely disturbing dream sequence which we later discover to be John Merrick's recurring nightmare: a fluid jumble of half-seen images, stunningly shot in black and white by Freddie Francis (as is the entire film), conjures up the old wives' tale that his mother was frightened during pregnancy by circus elephants in the streets of Leicester. These images of a woman in childbirth menaced by wild elephants hover over the film with their reminder that civilisation and the jungle are worlds apart.

We then set out, with the distinguished surgeon Treves (Anthony Hopkins), in quest of the hideous freak whom he means to exhibit, in furtherance of his career, as a medical curiosity.

The film provides Merrick (John Hurt) with an elaborate and remarkably effective make-up based on contemporary photographs; and cunningly delayed by shadows and a discreet hood, our first full-faced glimpse is a superbly calculated shock.

The way in which Merrick visibly blooms into his discovery of love, friendship, poetry and romance – into the joy of being human, in other words – is enormously moving. Beautifully written and directed, superbly acted, *The Elephant Man* is a genuinely remarkable film.

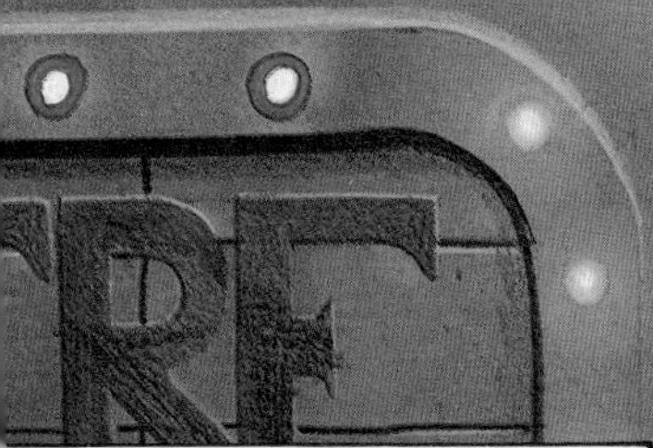

Jonathan Smith is establishing himself as a quietly effective novelist, and *In Flight*, his third novel, is a lively, poignant narrative about a young English academic who has left his wife waiting in Tennessee while he applies for a job at Bristol University. His June visit to England involves him with a boy who is dying of leukaemia in his brother's hospital, with his sister-in-law and her affectionate little daughter, and with their unhappily married friend Jane (whose monstrously chauvinist husband is briskly sketched).

The story's pace is urgent, Richard's feelings are vividly registered, and although there are some sentimental lapses in the love affair ('For always is always now'), the painfulness of the choices, the pressure of responsibilities not fully met, is acutely felt.

2. Now answer these questions about each review:

Macbeth

(i) How has the play been reviewed?
(ii) What word is used to describe the acting?
(iii) For what was the production 'notable'?
(iv) Who or what is described as being 'deranged'?

In Flight

(i) How many characters are involved in the story?
(ii) Who or what is described as:
(a) quietly effective? (b) lively and poignant? (c) briskly sketched?
(d) urgent? (e) vividly registered? (f) having sentimental lapses?
(iii) Which of the above is an unfavourable criticism?

The Elephant Man

(i) In which paragraph does the critic change from giving a neutral description to an opinion or reaction?
(ii) Which words and phrases help you to decide what the critic's opinion of the film is?

Xanadu

(i) What words does the critic use to describe:
(a) the story?
(b) the special effects?
(c) the quality of colour and sound?
(ii) Does the critic think that everyone will hate the film?

3. Make sensible sentences from this table:

Manhattan	is	superbly	sung
The part of Hedda Gabler	are	sentimentally	conducted
The desert shots	was	crudely	directed
The last aria of *La Bohème*	were	movingly	photographed
The pas de deux in *Swan Lake*		beautifully	portrayed
The new novel by Marilyn French		pretentiously	written
Village life in the 19th century		brilliantly	acted
Beethoven's Fifth Symphony			danced
			described

Change these sentences in the following way:

Manhattan was brilliantly directed.
The direction of *Manhattan* was brilliant.

6 Writing

In pairs or groups, discuss and then write a review of a play, television programme or a film that you have seen recently. Use this guide to assemble your notes before you write.

PARAGRAPH 1

Introduction
Factual information:
title/where seen/writer/director/
cast/other relevant details.

Sample guide: 'A play I saw recently on television was the BBC's production of Shakespeare's *Romeo and Juliet.* It was directed by Jack Good and starred John Duttine and Francesca Annis in the leading roles.'

PARAGRAPH 2

Main contents (i)
Descriptive information:
the period/the setting/ the characters/the story.

Sample guide: 'The play was surprisingly performed in modern dress and was set in present-day Italy. Romeo and Juliet are the two main characters. Romeo is the son of . . .'

PARAGRAPH 3

Main contents (ii)
Your reactions:
favourable or unfavourable reactions to acting/ direction/costumes/photography etc.

Sample guide: 'On the whole I enjoyed the play, but I thought that the second half was not as effective as the first. The play seemed to lose its dramatic pace. Although the leading roles were particularly well-acted, the supporting cast were rather weak. This, in my opinion, spoilt the overall quality of the production.'

PARAGRAPH 4

Conclusion
Your recommendations:
Would you/wouldn't you recommend people to see it?

Sample guide: 'In spite of my criticisms, I found this production interesting and moving. If you like productions of Shakespeare in modern dress, this one is, in my view, well worth seeing.'

7 Listening

Gerry has just returned from the cinema. He calls in to see Judy. Listen and then list all Gerry's arguments for going to see *films* in one column, and all Judy's arguments for preferring *books* in another, like this:

GERRY: FOR FILMS	JUDY: FOR BOOKS
More real; better atmosphere because of photography, costumes etc.	Can use own imagination to create a picture

When you have completed the two lists, decide which of the two you support and write a paragraph making and illustrating this point. Start with either of these topic sentences:

'Seeing the film version of a story is far more satisfying, in my opinion, than reading the book of the same story.'

or 'Reading the book is far more satisfying, in my view, than seeing the film of the same story.'

Introduce your 1st reason with: For one reason . .
your 2nd reason with: Another reason is that . . .

and your 3rd/4th with: Furthermore . . .
Also, . . .

If you want to *contrast* something in, for example, the film with something in the book, you can say:
Whereas in the film . . . , in the book . . .
or In the film, ... In the book, *on the other hand,* . . .

8 Discussion

Can you think of:
- a film and a book of the same title?
- a pop tune sung by two different singers?
- anything else like this that you can compare?

Discuss your ideas and preferences with the rest of the group.

Oral exercises

1. Expressing taste (Open exercise)

I'm really keen on pop music. Are you?
Well, pop music isn't really my taste.

And I love landscape paintings. Do you?
Yes, that's just the sort of painting I like.

1. I adore horror films. Do you like them?
2. Classical music is my favourite. Do you listen to it much?
3. Are you like me – crazy about detective stories?
4. I think historical novels are fascinating. Do you ever read them?
5. Ah! abstract paintings. Do you like them too?

2. Talking about reviews

This reviewer says that it's the best production he's ever seen.
It's had a lot of good reviews, hasn't it?
On the radio, they said it was awful.
It's had a lot of bad reviews, hasn't it?

1. The critic in *The Times* thought it was really great.
2. 'A monumental bore,' it says here!
3. This one says it made her feel sick.
4. The chap on the TV said that he was glued to the screen.
5. Listen to this. 'This play should never have been staged.' Well!

3. Expressing critical opinion (1)

The acting wasn't too good.
Really? I thought it was very professionally acted, actually.

1. The dancing seemed a bit clumsy.
2. None of them seemed to be able to reach the top notes.
3. That article he wrote was a bit amateurish, I felt.
4. Well, she doesn't seem to have much idea about directing!
5. The photography in that film was a bit poor, I thought.

4. Expressing critical opinion (2)

They say *The Romans in Britain* isn't very good.
Yes, I heard it wasn't worth seeing.

Norman said he enjoyed the play at the Apollo.
Yes, I heard it was well worth seeing.

1. The film on at the Odeon has had very good reviews.
2. John said he left halfway through that new Stoppard play.
3. The new Woody Allen film sounds awful.
4. I'm longing to see the new production of *Othello*.
5. Peter O'Toole's *Macbeth* has had very bad reviews.

Unit 6 Study focus

Interaction

FUNCTION	STRUCTURE
1. Expressing taste	'too' + adj + 'for me'/ 'my taste'
2. Expressing critical opinion	using adverb e.g. 'it was beautifully photographed' using adjective e.g. 'the photography was beautiful'
3. Comparing and contrasting	comparison of adjectives and adverbs. 'whereas'/'on the other hand'/'for one reason'/ 'another reason is . . .' 'furthermore'/'also'

ADDITIONAL STRUCTURES
'well worth' + verb (ing)
'not worth'

Vocabulary
Verbs and expressions of taste
The creative arts: literature, theatre, films, music, ballet, opera, painting.

Writing skills
1. Note-taking under headings from text.
2. Guided, linked paragraphs about a painting you like.
3. Guided composition: a review of a film, TV programme or play.
4. Linked sentences: comparing and contrasting different media.

Unit 7 Explorer

Before you start:

Do you think there are any parts of the world which still remain unexplored?
What parts of the world would you like to explore?
What sort of people go exploring?
Would you make a good explorer?
Which famous explorers do you know about?

❶ Mary Kingsley

Name:	Mary Henrietta Kingsley
Date of birth:	13th October, 1862
Place of birth:	Islington, London
Died:	3rd June, 1900 of enteric fever, Cape Town, South Africa
Occupation:	Explorer and writer
Education:	At home, reading father's books
Home life:	Mother an invalid, father often travelled; nursed mother and father. Both died in 1892
Interests:	Reading and studying scientific subjects: chemistry, ethnography, anthropology and natural history
Early travel:	Paris, 1888; Canaries, 1892
First journey of exploration:	Tropical West Africa, 1893–4
Second journey of exploration:	Tropical West Africa, including the Ogowe River and Mount Cameroon
Major publications:	*Travels in West Africa,* 1897 *West African Studies,* 1899

Check

How long ago did Mary Kingsley live?
What was she famous for?
In which part of the world did she concentrate her work?
On the map, find the places mentioned.

1. Write questions for each piece of information given in the chart above, like this:

What was Mary Kingsley's full name?
When and where was she born?

Using the questions and the information, ask and answer questions about Mary Kingsley, in pairs.

2. By the time she was 20, she had read all her father's books on science.

Make more statements like this about Mary Kingsley and her life. Use these key words in the statements:

26/travelled/Paris
30/travelled/Paris and the Canaries
30/both parents/died
32/explored Tropical West Africa once
died/written two books/made second journey of exploration to . . .

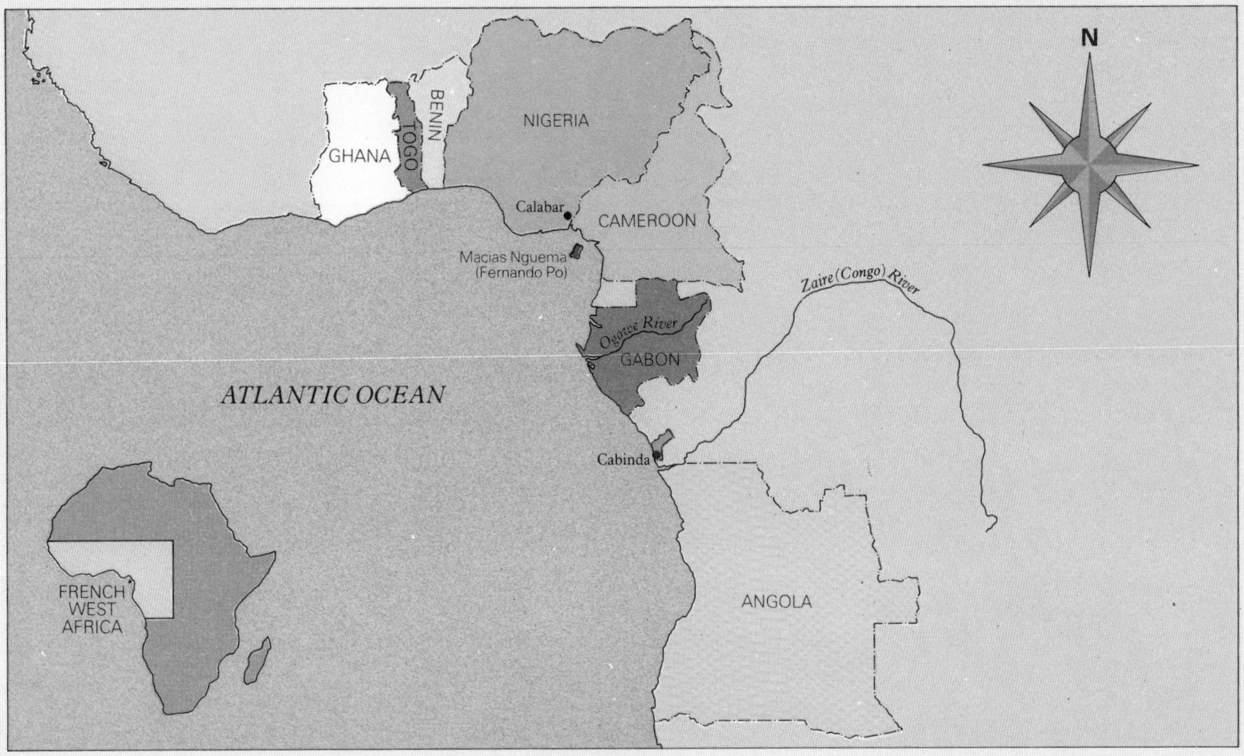

N
GHANA
TOGO
BENIN
NIGERIA
Calabar
CAMEROON
Macias Nguema
(Fernando Po)
Zaire (Congo) River
Ogowe River
GABON
ATLANTIC OCEAN
Cabinda
ANGOLA
FRENCH
WEST
AFRICA

KINGSLEY, MARY HENRIETTA
(1862-1900), traveller and writer, born in Islington on 13th October 1862, was the only daughter and eldest child of Dr George Henry Kingsley by his wife, Mary Bailey.

Her parents removed to Highgate in 1863, soon after her birth, and there she passed her first sixteen years. She had a somewhat irregular home-training, among books, quiet domestic duties, the care of numerous pet animals and a rambling garden.

She was not sent to school or college, but read omnivorously, and in truth had a world of her own amid the old books of travel, natural history, works on science, country sport, and literature, which she found on her father's shelves. The family led a retired life, and Mary grew up a shy, rather silent girl, disliking social gatherings.

Her father was an enthusiastic traveller with keen scientific interests. These his daughter fully shared. She was fond of natural history, especially of her father's favourite study of fishes and their ways. She learned German, but not French, which later she regretted.

3. What new information do you learn about Mary Kingsley from this text?

4. There are several words in the text which are rather old-fashioned or which are often used in literary texts. Below are more common expressions. Find their equivalents in the text.

moved (e.g. house)	many	in fact
spent (of time)	large and wild	quiet
rather unusual	widely	parties
jobs round the house	among	
education		

Now write out the text from 'Her parents' to 'social gatherings' using these words instead.

5. Imagine that Mary Kingsley had been born in 1982 instead of 1862. How would her life have been different? In pairs, discuss and then complete these statements:

She	would could (n't) might	have......	school university the house parents an explorer West Africa enteric fever

2

1. Imagine that you were exploring these regions. What do you think would be the dangers facing you?

These words below may give you clues. Group them first into the region to which they apply, like this:
desert or jungle: thirst

thirst	snakebite	dangerous ravines
sunstroke	sunburn	lions and tigers
frostbite	blizzards	mosquitoes
	avalanches	disease

2. Now ask and answer questions like this:

Supposing you were exploring in the desert, what would you be afraid of?

I'd be afraid of:
– running out of water and dying of thirst: getting lost/ dying of . . .

Look at the following 'Basic Survival Kit'. In pairs or groups, decide which items you would need for an exploratory expedition in the four regions: desert, jungle, arctic and mountain. Say why you would (or would not) need each item, like this:

A compass would be useful:
– in case you lost your way.
– to tell you where you were.

- Matches (in a waterproof container that will not break if stepped on or fallen on)
- Knife (sheath type in a leather case)
- Compass
- Small first-aid kit (sticking plasters, bandages, antiseptic, Disprin or Anadin)
- Snakebite kit (for regions with poisonous snakes)
- Lightweight nylon cord
- Whistle
- Torch
- Metal mirror
- Paper and pencil
- Water purifying tablets (from a chemist)
- Fishing line and hooks
- Space-blanket (lightweight protective blanket)

Now choose one of the areas and put in order of priority the items which you would need. Discuss your results with the other pairs or groups afterwards.

desert regions

arctic regions

jungle regions

mountain regions

4 Writing

Nowadays exploration expeditions rely heavily on the support of commerce and industry to help pay for equipment and supplies. Choose an expedition and a product you think you will need (some sort of food or drink, or a space-blanket). Write a letter to the firm which manufactures this product, asking for sponsorship and financial support.

Organise your letter in two paragraphs, like this:

	Dear Sir,
Topic sentence	Where you are going and when
	Why you are going How you are travelling How long you think the expedition will take
Topic sentence	You would like the firm to sponsor you
	Why the firm's product will be useful Why financial support is necessary What benefit the firm will get
	I look forward to hearing from you. Yours faithfully,

❺ Marco Polo

Venice at the time of Marco Polo

Read the passage and then complete the biographical details in the chart.

Marco Polo was a Venetian traveller, whose descriptions of his journey across the world from Venice to China and back, and of his experiences in the vast dominions of the Mongol emperor Kublai, make one of the greatest books of all time. This remarkable work, *The Book of Marco Polo, Citizen of Venice, Called Million, Wherein Is Recounted the Wonders of the World,* is a forerunner of scientific geography. Its author was the first to inform the West of the extent and power of China, and the first to give an intelligible account of the ways there.

Marco Polo was born either at Venice, or perhaps at Korcula (Curzola), a Venetian outpost on an island off the Dalmatian coast, in 1254. His father, Niccolo Polo, and his father's brother, Matteo, were members of a noble family of Dalmatian origin. They were merchants and had commercial interests in Constantinople. From there they set out, in 1261, on a long trading expedition which led them ultimately to the court of Kublai, the Great Khan who ruled over China. After seven years they returned to Italy, carrying letters from the Khan to the Pope.

Two years passed before the brothers resolved to start again on their travels, and this time, they took with them Niccolo's son Marco, then 17 years old. They travelled to Acre and from there rode overland to Hormuz on the Persian Gulf. From there they turned northward and made their way through Persia to Balkh, and Khotan. From Khotan they passed near Lop Nor, crossed the Gobi Desert and entered China by way of Su-chou. At length, in 1275, after a journey lasting three years, they presented themselves to Kublai Khan at his summer palace at Shang-tu.

Marco records that he made rapid progress in the Great Khan's favour; he studied the Mongol language and was entrusted by the emperor with various missions to different parts of his realm. As he became an astute man of business, Marco made careful notes of his itineraries, the state of the cities, the customs of the people, and the kinds of crops and other products. After 17 years travelling in the service of the Khan, Marco, together with his father and uncle, obtained leave to return to Venice. The journey took them 3 years and they arrived in 1295.

Marco could not remain inactive and in 1298 he is reported as being commander of a Venetian warship. In battle against the Genoese, he was taken prisoner. His few months as prisoner of war were the reason for his book. While in prison, he met Rusticiano of Pisa, to whom he dictated the story of his adventures. He returned to Venice after a year and died there in January 1324.

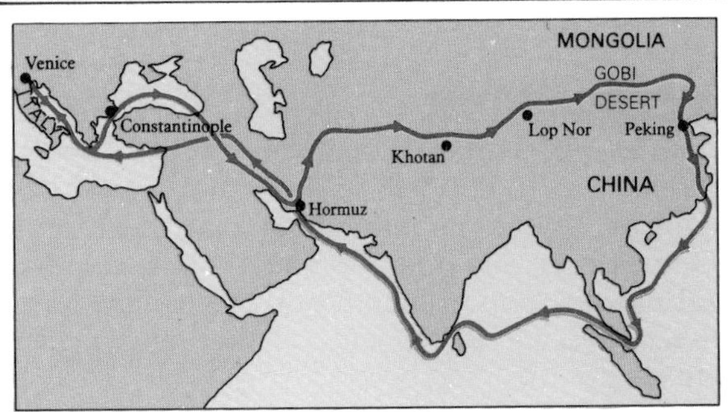

Date of birth: ....
Place of birth: ....
Father's occupation: ....
Main achievement: ....

Important events and dates:

1261	....
......	Father returned to Italy.
1270	....
......	The Venetians arrived at the emperor's summer palace.
......	They left China for Venice.
1295	....
1298	....
......	He returned to Venice.
1324	Marco Polo died at the age of 70.

These are some of the things Marco Polo wrote about the places he visited in ancient China.

MONGOLIA

In every house there is a figure of the earth-god, whom they honour and worship.
The Tartar soldiers carry no gear with them except a leather bottle of milk, a little earthenware pot to cook their meat in, and a little tent to shelter them from the rain.

SHANG-TU

Here the Great Khan keeps 10,000 horses. The milk of the mares is for the Khan himself. No-one else dares to touch it.

KHANBALIK

The Great Khan has priests of many religions about him.
The emperor's pleasure park is planted with beautiful trees from all corners of the empire.
The Khan uses paper money made from the bark of the mulberry tree.
Women here share an equal place with men, except in matters of hunting and war.
The walls of the palace are covered with brilliantly coloured reliefs.

TAIAN-FU

Here iron is mined, smelted and treated by ironsmiths for the armaments of the imperial army.

SINGAN-FU

Here they weave cloth of gold ... the price is very reasonable.

CHINGKIANG

Here there are two Christian churches.

TIBET

Paper money is not used here; instead, salt is the main currency.

HANGCHOW

Several thousand excellent communal baths, each big enough for 100 persons.
Each day some four tonnes of pepper are consumed in this city. The Khan levies a tax of 33⅓% on salt and spices and 10% on silk.

KARAJAN

Many people here eat their meat raw, chopped with garlic and spice.
... dangerous serpents and alligators all around us.

ZARDANDAN

After a woman has given birth to a child, her husband takes to his bed with the child beside him for five or six weeks.

MIEN

... pagodas covered with gold and silver and hung with bells tinkling in the wind.

KWEICHAU

We are constantly on guard against fierce lions.

KWANGSI

The people here burn their dead and put the ashes in caverns in the mountains.

FOOCHOW

... fine pottery at very low prices.

FUKIEN

In these mountains, wild men carry spears and eat human flesh.

About 200 years after Marco Polo's voyage, Christopher Columbus sailed westward on the Atlantic Ocean, hoping to find China. He took with him a heavily annotated copy of Marco Polo's book.

1. Marco Polo was a person of great ability and character. He also had an enquiring mind. Read the quotations from his journals on China on the previous page. Find three examples to illustrate each of the following points:

He was an extremely observant man with an eye for minute detail.
He was very interested in the religious practices of each place he visited.
He appreciated beautiful things.
He faced hardship and danger readily.
He was fascinated by people and their customs and by the structure of their societies.

2. Take three of the points and write a paragraph about each. Use each point as a topic sentence. Join your sentences together, like this:

Marco Polo faced hardship and danger readily. For instance, he tells us that in Kweichau they were constantly on guard against fierce lions. Furthermore, he reports that, in the mountains of Fukien, there were wild men who carried spears and ate human flesh. He also mentions that, in Karajan, dangerous serpents and alligators were all around them.

Topic sentence	Marco Polo faced hardship and danger readily	
1st example	for instance for example	he notes he observes he records he mentions he tells us he reports
2nd and 3rd examples	furthermore moreover also	

that

evidence provided by quotation

6 Listening

Peter Fraenkel is the author of a book called *Overland* – a practical guide to the organisation of overland expeditions. Here he talks about expeditions in the Sahara. Listen and note what advice he gives about the following topics: fuel, water, mechanical breakdown, camping equipment, clothes and medical supplies.

Oral exercises

1. Referring to events in the past

John is asking Helen about her past life.
Did you learn to type before you left school?
Oh yes, I'd learnt to type by then.

1. Did you move to Nottingham before you left school?
2. Did you start at the university before you got your flat?
3. Did you get a degree before you got married?
4. Did you get married before you went abroad?
5. Did you have the baby before you got this job?

Extra work

Re-express the answers like this:
Oh yes, by the time I left school I had learnt to type.

2. Hypothesising about dangers (Open exercise)

What would you do if you were in the jungle and you saw a lion?
I'd run away.

1. What would you do if you trod on a snake?
2. What would you do if a poisonous snake bit you?
3. What would you do if you came across a herd of elephants?
4. What would you do if you ran out of water in the desert?
5. What would you do if you got frostbite on top of a mountain?
6. What would you do if you lost your way in a dark forest?

3. Expressing fear (Open exercise)

Why might you be afraid of going on an expedition across the Sahara?
I'd be afraid of running out of water.

1. Why might you be afraid of going for a walk in a dark forest?
2. Why might you be afraid of going for an expedition through a jungle?
3. Why might you be afraid of meeting a tiger face to face?
4. Why might you be afraid of climbing Mount Everest?
5. Why might you be afraid of climbing a tall tree?
6. Why might you be afraid of canoeing up the Amazon?

4. Expressing purpose (Open exercise)

Nerris is taking the family on a hiking and camping trip. Her daughter is with her as she checks the equipment.

NERRIS: Oh, good, there's the compass.
CHILD: What's the compass for?
NERRIS: *For helping us to find the way.*
CHILD: What's the groundsheet for?
NERRIS: *For keeping our sleeping bags dry.*

1. What's the compass for?
2. What's the groundsheet for?
3. What's the mosquito net for?
4. What's the paper and pencil for?
5. What's the whistle for?

Unit 7 Study focus

Interaction

FUNCTION	STRUCTURE
1. Linking two events in the past	'by the time' . . . + past perfect
2. Hypothesising about a person's past life	3rd conditional: 'would(n't) have' . . . 'might(n't) have' + verb
3. Hypothesising about possible dangers	2nd conditional: 'I'd be afraid of' + verb (ing)
4. Expressing purpose and precaution	'to' + infinitive 'for' + verb (ing) 'in case' + past simple

Vocabulary

Education and academic subjects
Equipment for travel and exploration
Natural hazards
Ancient civilisation

Writing skills

1. Sentence completion using key verbs
2. Text reconstruction
3. Sentence completion using key words
4. Guided formal letter of request
5. Guided paragraphs: topic sentence plus supporting evidence, using linking devices

Unit 8 A case for treatment

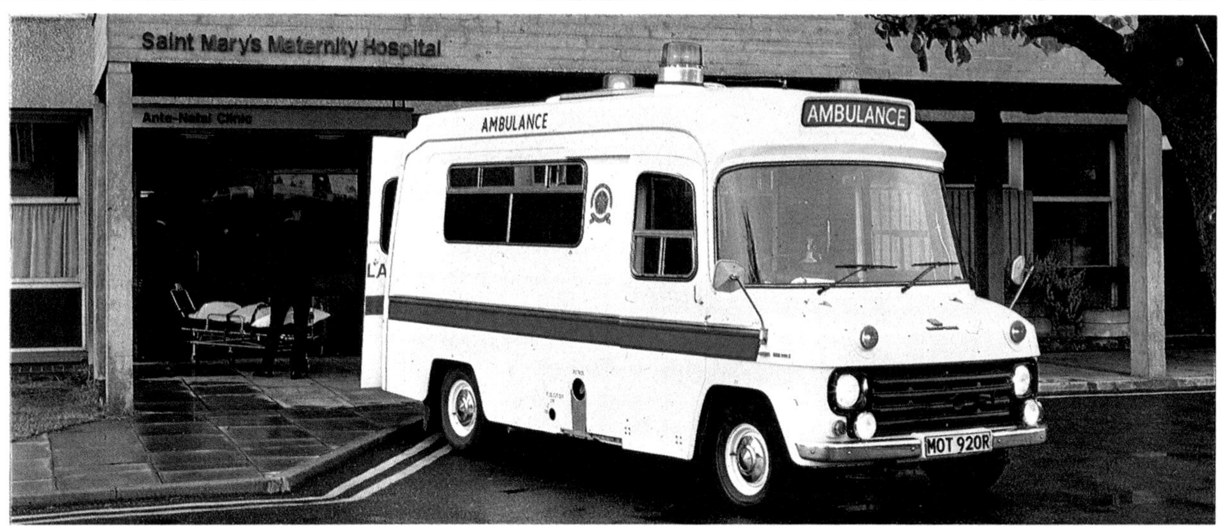

Before you start:

Have you ever been in hospital for more than a day?
Which parts of the hospital routine did (or would) you find difficult?
Which advances in modern medicine do you admire most?

1 [cassette]

Lynne Williams is 38. She runs a dry cleaning business with her husband, Ted. She has always thought of herself as a healthy person but a few days ago she started getting pains in her stomach. One morning her husband noticed her bending over the counter in obvious pain.

TED: Is anything the matter?
LYNNE: No, it's all right. Just a slight pain in my side.
TED: Why don't you sit down for a moment?
LYNNE: No, don't fuss. It doesn't hurt very much. I'll be all right in a minute.

But all that day the pain grew worse. Lynne was sick several times and had a temperature well above normal. Finally she decided to call the doctor. The doctor examined her and diagnosed appendicitis. He said she had to go into hospital immediately and have her appendix removed.

Check

Why did Lynne call the doctor?
What was wrong with her?
Why did she have to go into hospital?

1. Practise the conversation between Lynne and Ted in pairs. Then practise it a few more times, each time changing the part of the body **where the pain is centred, e.g.** shoulder, neck, ear, foot, ankle, waist, hip.

Example: Is anything the matter?
No, it's all right. Just a slight pain in my back.

2. [cassette]

Fill in Lynne's part of her conversation with the doctor. Read it in pairs.

DOCTOR: Now, Mrs Williams. What seems to be the matter?
LYNNE: ....
DOCTOR: Let me have a look ... Mm ... does it hurt when I press here?
LYNNE: ....
DOCTOR: When did this pain start?
LYNNE: ....
DOCTOR: Have you been sick at all?
LYNNE: ....
DOCTOR: Have you been feeling feverish?
LYNNE: ....
DOCTOR: Well, I'm afraid you've got appendicitis. We must get you into hospital at once and have that appendix removed.

3. Lynne goes home and tells her husband about her visit to the doctor. She reports what the doctor asked, what she replied and what she diagnosed. Prepare and act their conversation.

4. Read the piece below about appendicitis from a medical handbook and find alternative terms for:

stomach
temperature
sign
beat of blood
being sick

> *Appendicitis*
>
> Infection of the appendix. The first symptom of an acute appendicitis is pain in the abdomen around the navel. As the infection spreads the pain moves to the lower right quadrant. Vomiting usually accompanies the pain, with slight fever and rapid pulse. The best treatment in most cases, once a doctor is sure of the diagnosis, is removal of the inflamed appendix.

5. Listening

Complete the doctor's notes on Lynne. Use medical terms where possible. Then listen to the doctor talking to two other patients. Complete the missing information in the notes.

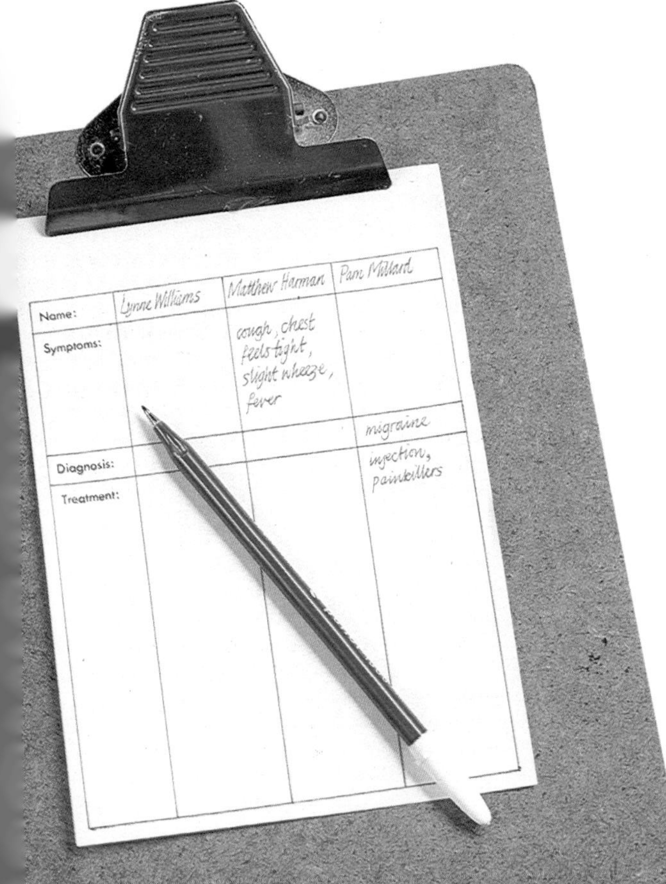

❷ What happens in hospitals?

1. Group the following words under the appropriate verb:

TAKE REMOVE TEST

temperature appendix tooth eyes pulse tonsils X-ray ears

2. Look at the pictures below and say what is happening in each, like this:

Picture 1: He's having his temperature taken.

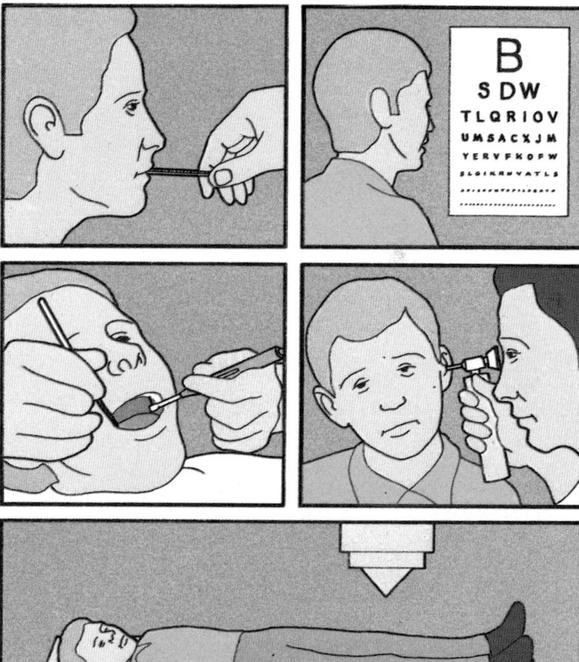

3. Ask and answer in pairs:

Have you ever had your appendix or tonsils removed?
Have you ever had your eyes or ears tested?
Have you ever had your pulse taken by a nurse or doctor?

Discussion

When you were a child, did you ever have . . .
food poisoning?
scarlet fever?
chicken pox?
measles?
whooping cough?

What was it like? What were the symptoms? How long did it take you to recover?

Before you start:

What sort of things do you think you should take with you if you are going into hospital for some time?
In what ways can your family and friends help you?
Why is the daily routine in hospital different from home for most people?
Can you think of any advice that you should give to patients when they go into hospital?

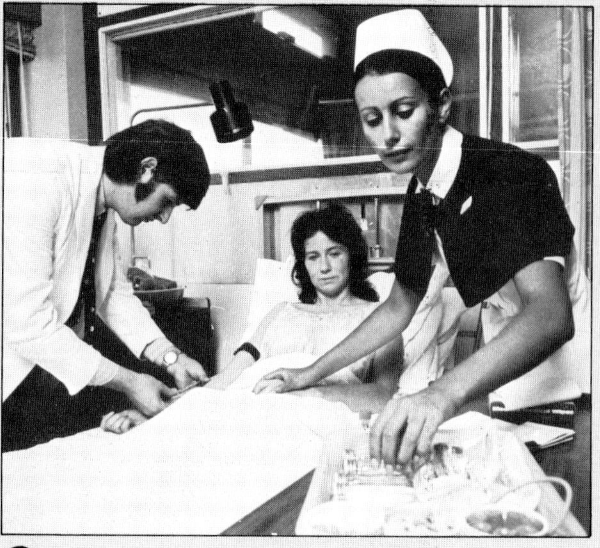

1. Read the Guidelines for Patients **and decide what rules and restrictions exist in the General Hospital in Weymouth. Rewrite them using the language in the box below. Compare your list with your partner's.**

RULES:
You have to ...
You should ...
You're supposed to ...

RESTRICTIONS:
You're not allowed to ...
You're not supposed to ...
They'd rather you (didn't) ...

2. Work in pairs. It is your first day in hospital. Your partner has been in hospital for several weeks. You ask him/her about the hospital rules, like this:

- Who does our washing?
- You're supposed to ask a friend or relative to do it for you.

Make up some questions like these and answer them.

- What's the food like?
- I've only got my nightwear and toilet things with me. What else do I need?

3. You have now been in hospital for over a week. You find it difficult to get used to the rules and restrictions. Make remarks to your partner, starting like this:

I just can't get used to (the hospital food).
I usually ...
(waking up so early). I ...
(not being allowed to ...)

Guidelines for patients

from the Hospital Secretary Weymouth General Hospi

You help us and we'll help you to get better sooner!

Personal belongings

Remember that when you come hospital there is never a great dea cupboard space, so don't bring tc many belongings with you. You should bring your own nightwe pyjamas or nightdresses; toilet ar and some small change for newspapers and for any other ite you may require from the hospit shop. Finally, don't forget your medical documents. They are essential.

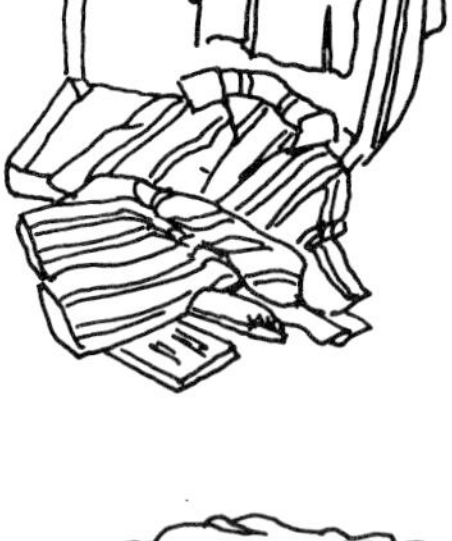

Washing

It is a great help if you can arrang a relative or friend to bring you regular changes of nightwear an clean clothes you require.

Meals

It is very important for you to bu up and keep your strength while are in hospital. Please try to eat a your meals.

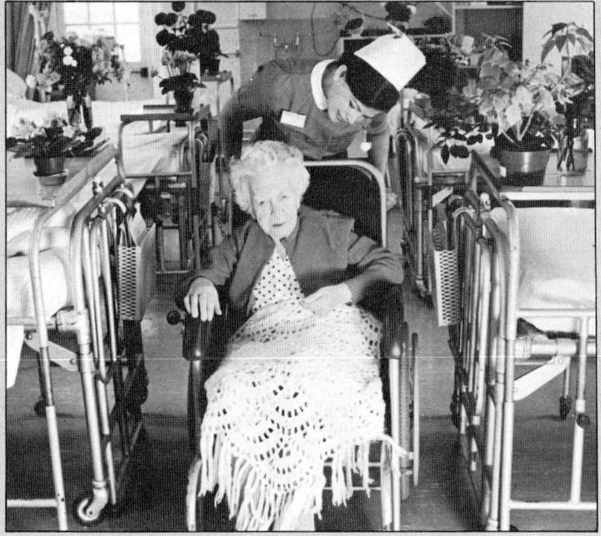

Hospital hours

You'll find that the daily routine in hospital is different from what you are used to at home. The day begins much earlier – usually at about 6am and ends earlier too: bedtime is at about 9.30pm. Breakfast is at 8am, lunch at 12 noon, afternoon tea at 3.30pm and supper at 6pm.

Telephoning

Please don't ask more than one person to telephone the hospital each day to find out how you are. Ask them to pass on the news about you to your relatives and friends.

Smoking and drinking

Please observe the 'No Smoking' signs in the wards. Your Ward Sister will tell you about our restrictions concerning smoking. Alcoholic beverages are strictly forbidden.

Visitors

Visiting hours are 2.30-3.30pm and 7-8pm. Make sure that your friends and relatives know when they can come to visit you. Remember only two visitors round the bed at a time! Visitors with any signs of a cold, flu or other infectious illnesses are not allowed in the wards.

4. Writing

Write short letters for the following situations:

(i) You have forgotten to bring some personal belongings with you into hospital. Write to a friend or relative asking for the things you need.

(ii) Write to your teacher, asking him/her to tell your classmates that you are ill in hospital, and to explain to them about visiting times and telephone calls.

Note: For *making requests* use:
'Do you think you could . . .?'
'Would you mind . . .ing?'

5. Writing

You are in charge of a group of campers on a summer holiday. Write a notice called Guidelines for Perfect Campers, which you will send out to everyone before the holiday. Use these headings:

Equipment and clothes (tent/groundsheet etc.)
Personal belongings
Washing
Meal times
Fire hazards

Accidents at work can often be very dangerous. Sometimes people can lose a hand, an arm or a leg in an industrial accident. What can doctors do about this sort of accident nowadays?

Read this article about a baby involved in an accident with a tractor.

Fight to save baby's arm

A baby was undergoing micro-surgery last night in a bid to save an arm, after his pram was crushed by a tractor.

Twenty-two-month-old Ryan Millard of Dalton, Cumbria, was rushed 100 miles to Manchester's Withington Hospital after the accident near his home.

The operation involved a specialist team of surgeons who have sewn back arms on two patients at the hospital in the past five weeks.

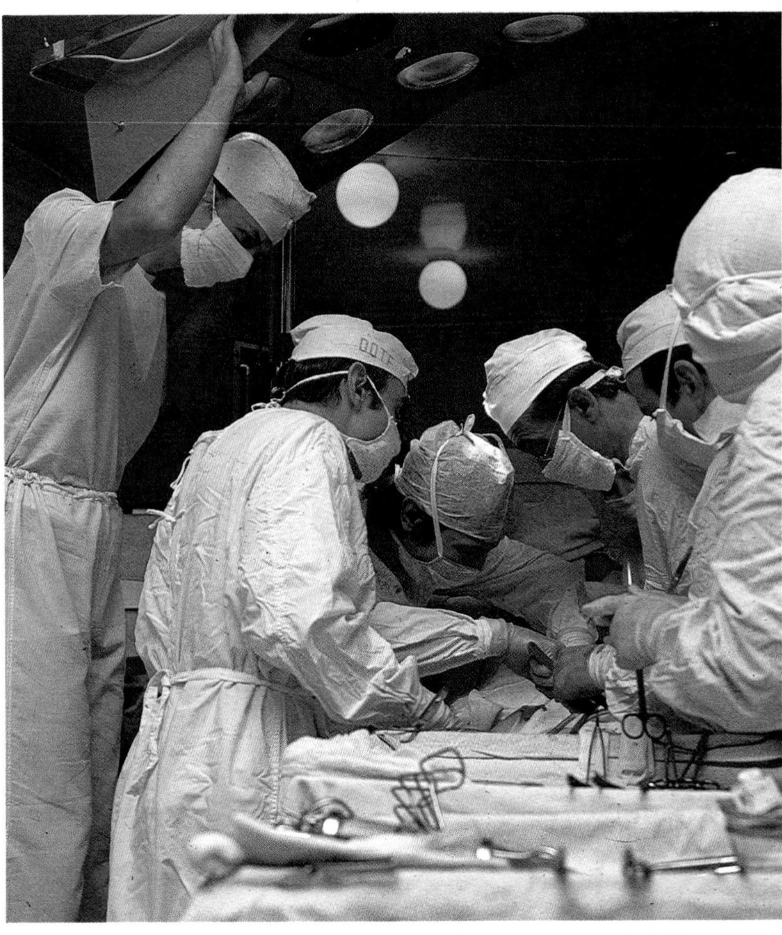

Check

What happened to the baby's arm?

How were doctors going to save it?

Read this more detailed account of the operation on the baby's arm.

The miracle that saved a baby's arm

It took more than ten hours for five surgeons and two anaesthetists, working through the night, to sew back Ryan Millard's left arm.

The 22-month-old baby woke up only minutes after the operation, doctors said. Now his parents wait to see if the incredibly complex and difficult operation has been a complete success.

After Ryan's arm had been severed in two places, the two parts were packed in ice for the journey to Withington. Ice keeps a severed limb viable for valuable hours longer so that surgeons have a chance to sew it back.

Now Ryan has gone through all this, what are his chances of making a complete recovery? About 60-40, the doctors said.

Hospital secretary, Mr David Astley, said yesterday, 'The operation was technically successful, but it will be some months before we know whether the baby will have 100 percent use of his arm.'

Ryan's mother, Mrs Glynis Millard, said, 'We are so grateful to the doctors who have performed this miracle.'

The best meaning of 'complex' is:

(a) tiring (b) complicated (c) expensive.

The best meaning of 'severed' is:

(a) injured (b) cut (c) bruised (d) cut off.

The best meaning of 'viable' is:

(a) usable (b) uninfected (c) cool.

Check

How long did the operation take?

Why was it still possible to use the baby's severed arm?

Was the operation completely successful?

Why do you think the operation was complex?

Why do you think five surgeons were needed?

Now read in the text below how the operation is carried out:

Re-write the process like this:

1. First they shave back the bone and then pin the bones together.
2. Then they . . .
3. After that, . . .
4. Finally . . .

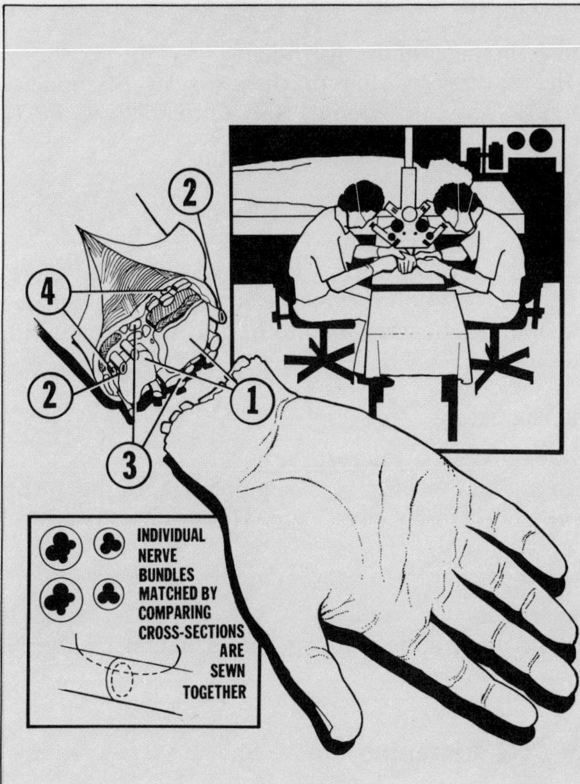

How microsurgeons sew back a severed hand: 1. Bone shaved back to avoid contaminated bone and allow for shortening of blood vessels. Bones pinned together. 2. Main vein and artery sewn together to re-establish blood flow. 3. Tendons that bend and straighten the thumb and fingers stitched together. 4. Wound reopened after 8-12 weeks, grown nerve bundles matched and sewn together, sometimes grafting nerves from the leg.

Microsurgery has always been long and arduous – one operation at Withington Hospital, Manchester, on Thursday, lasted 19 hours, which must be something of a record. But the task of joining arteries and veins, only half a millimetre in diameter, has been immeasurably eased by the development of a new microscope, with two or even three heads, that allows additional surgeons to work on the severed part at once.

The last two years have also seen the development of finer stitching materials, more effective drugs to prevent clotting, better anaesthesia techniques – important when a patient is to be kept 'under' for 19 hours – improved physiotherapy, and better selection of patients suitable for the operation in the first place.

5

The high cost of limb repair

Limb replacement can take from eight to 20 hours. It needs a surgical team of six, anaesthetists, nurses and assistants. The patient then needs several weeks of care in hospital and several months of physiotherapy. He may need further operations. It is difficult to calculate the cost of such an operation because there are so many variables, but surgeons and DHSS administrators agree that £20,000 would not be far wrong. In a time of cuts in the National Health Service, is it worth it? Even the best surgeons have their doubts. Cobbett says, 'It's unlikely that a patient will regain sufficient sensitivity in the hand to tell the difference between a coin and a paper clip, and the hand will be capable only of relatively coarse movement.' Another surgeon says, 'I remain to be convinced that a hand sewn back is more useful than an artificial limb.'

Check

Why is this type of operation so expensive?
In what way is the operation unlikely to be completely effective?

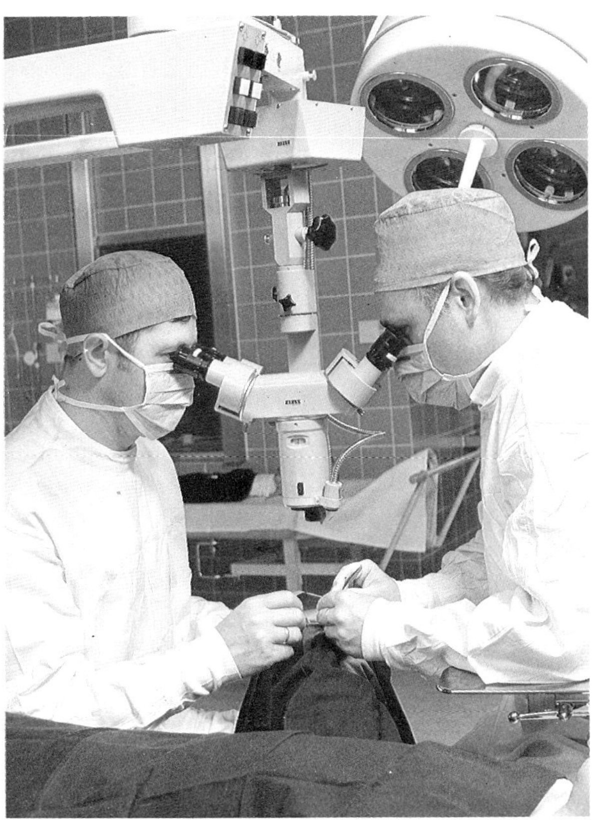

1. Make notes on the articles you have read. Use these headings:

MICROSURGERY

The four stages of the operation:
(i) Bone shaved back
(ii) ....
(iii) ....
(iv) ....

Recent developments:
(i) New microscope with 2/3 heads
(ii) ....
(iii) ....
(iv) ....
(v) ....
(vi) ....

Disadvantages of microsurgery:
(i) Cost
(a) Long operation and large team needed
(b) ....
(c) ....
(ii) ....

2. When you have completed your notes, write a composition about microsurgery, using your own words as far as possible. Use this guide.

PARAGRAPH 1

Introduction

True life story of Ryan Millard
'Not long ago 22-month-old Ryan Millard had his arm crushed by a tractor. Ten hours after the accident the arm was sewn back by a team of microsurgeons.'

PARAGRAPH 2

The four stages of the operation
'Microsurgery is one of the miracles of modern surgery. The operation consists of four stages. First, . . .'

PARAGRAPH 3

Recent developments
'Microsurgery has existed for some time but there have been several recent developments which make the operation easier and more likely to succeed. For example . . .'

PARAGRAPH 4

Disadvantages of microsurgery
'There are, however, certain points against the use of microsurgery on a large scale. These are . . .'

PARAGRAPH 5

Conclusion
To sum up, in spite of the problems that microsurgery presents, in my opinion . . .

6 Listening

Listen to this doctor talking about National Health versus private medicine in Britain. Note down two arguments *against* and two *for* private medicine. Note also his own personal opinion.

Oral exercises

1. Explaining what is wrong with you

Is anything the matter?
No, just a slight pain in my shoulder. I'll be all right in a minute.

1. right arm	3. chest	5. ankle
2. back	4. elbow	6. wrist

2. Giving advice about treatment

There's something wrong with my eyes, I think. I can't seem to see too well.
You'd better have them tested then.

My appendix is causing me trouble again.
You'd better have it removed then.

I think I may have broken my leg.
You'd better have it X-rayed then.

1. I can't hear very well. I think there may be something wrong with my ears.
2. I think I may have broken my arm.
3. The dentist says my wisdom tooth is dead.
4. My throat's very sore again. I think it's my tonsils.
5. I'm not sure if I've fractured my wrist or not.

3. Asking about health

I've got another cold!
Oh, do you suffer badly from colds?

1. I think Elsa has got another attack of migraine coming on.
2. Oh dear, my eyes are watering again. The pollen count must be high today.
3. I had another sleepless night last night.
4. We never go to see my parents now. The children always feel ill in the car.
5. Atishoo! Oh, not again! That's the third cold this winter.

4. Talking about habits

Two patients are talking in a hospital.

I don't like waking up at 6 am.
No, I can never get used to waking up at 6 either.

1. having breakfast so early
2. sleeping in an open ward
3. going to sleep at 9 pm.

Extra work

Complete each response like this:
I'm used to waking up . . .'

5. Talking about rules and restrictions

Two young people are staying in a youth hostel. These are some of the rules:

> Turn out the dormitory lights at 10 pm.
> Do not eat or drink in the dormitories.
> Do not smoke anywhere.
> Hand in all valuables to the warden.
> Put your bicycles in the shed at night.

Let's read a bit longer. It's only just gone ten.
Well, we're supposed to turn out the lights at ten, so perhaps we'd better not.

Let's have some coke and some crisps then.
Well, we're not supposed to eat or drink in the dormitories, so perhaps we'd better not.

1. Let's have a cigarette.
2. Let's keep our passports in our drawers. It's useful to have them around.
3. Let's leave our bikes here. I'm too tired to put them away.

Unit 8 Study focus

Interaction

FUNCTION	STRUCTURE
1. Asking and talking about ill health and symptoms	'Is anything the matter?' 'a pain in my . . .'
2. Asking about and describing treatment	'to have something done'
3. Talking about rules and restrictions	'(not) supposed to . . .' 'should' 'they'd rather you didn't . . .' 'have to . . .'/'not allowed to'
4. Talking about habits	'be used to' + verb (ing) 'usually' + present simple

ADDITIONAL STRUCTURE
'had better (not)' + verb

Vocabulary

Health: symptoms, diseases and illnesses
Parts of the body
Medical terms

Writing skills

1. Guided informal letter of request and explanation of rules
2. Notice (guidelines) for campers
3. Linked sentences: describing a process using sequencers
4. Guided composition – under headings using sequencers and cohesive devices

Unit 9 Celebration

Before you start:

What is your favourite celebration?
At what time of the year is it held?
Are there any festivals in your country which are associated with:
- a famous historical figure?
- a religious person or event?
- a particular season or time of year?

When do people give presents in your country?

❶ Mardi Gras

Pre-Lenten carnivals are still held in many places – for example in Rio de Janeiro, Nice, Binche and of course New Orleans. The carnival in New Orleans lasts for nearly two months and ends in the selection of a carnival king. These festivities reach their peak in the procession of splendid floats representing a theme that varies from year to year. Recently the procession included 29 floats representing the works of the science fiction writer, Jules Verne.

Check

Why do you think the carnival is held before Lent?
Do you think a float is: (a) something like a boat (b) dress or costume (c) a flat lorry or vehicle on wheels drawn in a procession?
Why does the Mardi Gras festival in New Orleans seem different from year to year?
How do the festivities end? Start your answer like this:
A carnival king . . .

Look at the photograph below and answer these questions:

What are the people doing? Where are they?
What time of day and what time of year do you think it is?
Why?
Describe the countryside. Which country do you think this might be?
What sort of special occasion do you think it is?

Now read this:

One of the most popular festivals of the year in Sweden *is* Midsummer's Eve, *which is celebrated on* the nearest Saturday to June 21st. This comes at the height of summer when the countryside is at its most beautiful. *The festival marks* the longest day of the year.

Several days before Midsummer's Eve, everyone helps to decorate a maypole, the symbol of midsummer. This is a tall mast decorated with birch leaves and wild flowers. *On the day of the festival,* the maypole is ceremoniously raised, usually in the middle of a field or meadow. While musicians, dressed in traditional costume, play folk music on fiddles and accordians, young and old alike sing and dance to traditional midsummer songs around the maypole.

In the evening, when the children have gone to bed, the dancing moves to a country barn or to a lakeside landing stage. In the north of Sweden, the sun hardly sets at this time of year. *Finally,* at about four or five in the morning, the dancing stops, the birds begin to sing and people wander wearily to bed. Midsummer *is over for another year.*

1. Make notes under these headings:

Name of festival: Country in which it takes place: Time of year: Reason for the festival: Preparation: The day of the festival (customs, dress, festivities and dancing): The evening of the festival:

2. Think of a popular festival in your country.

Write some sentences describing the events in sequence. Use these phrases:

The day before/after (the festival) . . .
In the morning/afternoon/ evening of . . .
At the end of (the day) . . .
When/after/before . . .
As soon as . . .

they | finish . . . / have finished . . .

Notice also these ways of talking about people:

Everybody / Everyone (wears) . . .
All the children (get up) . . .
Almost everyone (goes to church)
Most people / Some people (eat)
Each person/man/woman/child (has a . . .)
Hardly anyone (goes to bed)
Both the parents and the children (give . . .)

3 A dictionary of Christmas

Christ·mas /ˈkrɪsməs/ *n* [C;R] **1** also **Christmas Day** /ˌ·· ˈ·/— a Christian holy day usu. held on December 25th (or in some churches January 6th) in honour of the birth of Christ, usu. kept as a public holiday **2** the period just before, and the 12 days just after, this
Christmas cake /ˈ·· ·/ *n* [C;U] (a) heavy cake containing much dried fruit and usu. having a covering of ornamented hard sugar (ICING), made to be eaten at Christmas —compare CHRISTMAS PUDDING
Christmas card /ˈ·· ·/ *n* an ornamental GREETING CARD sent from one person to another at Christmas
Christmas Eve /ˌ·· ˈ·/ *n* [R] the day, and esp. the evening, before Christmas
Christmas pud·ding /ˌ·· ˈ··/ *n* [C;U] (a) heavy sweet dish (PUDDING) containing much dried fruit and often covered with burning alcohol (BRANDY), served esp. at the end of dinner on Christmas day —compare CHRISTMAS CAKE
Christmas stock·ing /ˌ·· ˈ··/ *n* a stocking (esp. hung by a fireplace or a bed) into which small CHRISTMAS presents are put (esp. for children)
Christ·mas·time /ˈkrɪsməstaɪm/ also (*lit*) **Christ·mas·tide** /-taɪd/— *n* [R] the period just before and the 12 days just after Christmas; the Christmas season
Christmas tree /ˈ·· ·/ *n* a real or man-made tree ornamented at Christmas with candles, lights, coloured paper, etc., often brought into the home
Father Christ·mas /ˌ·· ˈ··/ also (*esp. AmE*) **Santa Claus**— *n* [R] *esp. BrE* an imaginary old man in red clothes with a long white beard believed by children to come down the chimney at Christmas to bring their presents

Make one or two bi-lingual dictionary entries to do with a celebration in your country.

4 Conversation about Christmas

Dylan Thomas (1914–53), poet, short-story writer, radio playwright and journalist, was born in Swansea, in Wales. His poetry is powerful and full of life, although it is sometimes difficult to understand. Thomas had a great influence on the younger poets of his generation. Much of his work is autobiographical, and in the extract below he recalls what Christmas was like for him as a young boy in Wales.

Listen and read

SMALL BOY: Years and years and years ago, when you were a boy – what was Christmas like?
SELF: It snowed.
SMALL BOY: It snowed last year, too. I made a snowman and my brother knocked it down and I knocked my brother down and then we had tea.
SELF: But that was not the same snow. Our snow drifted out of the arms and hands and bodies of the trees; snow grew overnight on the roofs of the houses like moss and settled on the postman, opening the gate, like a thunderstorm of white torn Christmas cards.
SMALL BOY: Were there postmen, then, too?
SELF: They were just ordinary postmen, fond of walking, and dogs, and Christmas, and the snow. They knocked on the doors with blue knuckles –
SMALL BOY: And then the Presents?
SELF: And then the Presents. On Christmas Eve I hung at the foot of my bed a black stocking, and always, I said, I would stay awake all the moonlit, snowlit night to hear the roof-alighting reindeer and see the snowy boot descend through soot. But soon I was asleep before the chimney trembled and the room was red and white with Christmas. But in the morning, though no snow melted on the bedroom floor, the stocking bulged and brimmed: press it, it squeaked like a mouse-in-a-box; it smelt of tangerine.
SMALL BOY: Were there any sweets?
SELF: Of course there were sweets. And Easy Hobbi-Games. And a whistle to make the dogs bark. And, last of all, in the toe of the stocking, sixpence like a silver corn. And then downstairs for breakfast under the balloons!
SMALL BOY: What did you have for dinner?
SELF: Turkey, and blazing pudding.
SMALL BOY: Was it nice?
SELF: It was not made on earth.
SMALL BOY: What did you do after dinner?
SELF: The Uncles sat in front of the fire, took off their collars, loosened all buttons, put their large moist hands over their watch-chains, groaned a little, and slept. Mothers, aunts, and sisters scuttled to and fro, bearing tureens. The dog was sick. Auntie Beattie had to have three aspirins, but Auntie Hannah, who liked port, stood in the middle of the snowbound back-yard, singing like a big-bosomed thrush. I would blow up balloons to see how big they would blow up to; and, when they burst, which they all did, the Uncles jumped and rumbled. In the rich and heavy afternoon I would sit in the front room, among festoons and Chinese lanterns, and nibble at dates, and try to make a model man-o'-war. And then, at Christmas tea, the recovered Uncles would be jolly over their mince-pies; and the great iced cake loomed in the centre of the table like a marble grave. Auntie Hånnah laced her tea with rum, because it was only once a year. And in the evening, there was Music. An uncle played the fiddle, a cousin sang 'Cherry Ripe' and another uncle sang 'Drake's Drum'. It was very warm in the little house. Auntie Hannah, who had got on to the parsnip wine, sang a song about Rejected

Love, and then everybody laughed again, and then I went to bed. Looking through my bedroom window, out into the moonlight and the flying, unending, smoke-coloured snow, I could see the lights in the windows of all the other houses on our hill, and hear the music rising from them up the long, steadily falling night. I turned the gas down, I got into bed. I said some words to the close and holy darkness, and then I slept.

SMALL BOY: But it all sounds like an ordinary Christmas.
SELF: It was.
SMALL BOY: But Christmas when you were a boy wasn't any different to Christmas now.
SELF: It was, it was.
SMALL BOY: Why was Christmas different then?
SELF: I mustn't tell you. I mustn't tell you because it is Christmas now.

from: *A Prospect of the Sea,* short stories by Dylan Thomas

1. These are some of the author's memories of what he did at Christmas. Put them in the order in which they are mentioned in the text.

He found a sixpence in the toe of his stocking.
He sat in the front room and nibbled dates.
He hung his stocking at the foot of his bed. (1)
He went to bed after the music and the singing.
He tried to stay awake to see Father Christmas.
He said his prayers before going to sleep. (8)
He blew up balloons to see how big they would go.
He had breakfast under the balloons.

2.

> I remember I found a sixpence in the toe of my stocking.
> I remember *finding* a sixpence in the toe of my stocking.

Imagine you are the author. Look at the list of memories and say what you remember doing, like this:

I remember . . . ing . . .

3. What does the author remember about other people? Make a list, like this:

The Uncles sat in front of the fire after dinner and fell asleep.
Mothers, aunts and sisters . . .

Now express these memories like this:

I remember my uncles sitting . . . and falling . . .

Tell your partner and then write down some of the things you remember about your childhood.

4. Dylan Thomas writes in a figurative way: he uses metaphors and similes to make pictures.

metaphor:
'Our snow drifted out of the arms and hands and bodies of trees.' The trees don't really have arms, hands or bodies, but they look as if they do because of the branches and twigs.

simile:
'snow grew overnight on the roofs of houses *like* moss'.

The following descriptions are taken from the text. Try to explain them in your own words:

(i) . . . before the chimney trembled and the room was red and white with Christmas
(ii) . . . sixpence like a silver corn
(iii) . . . singing like a big-bosomed thrush
(iv) In the rich and heavy afternoon . . .
(v) . . . loomed like a marble grave . . .
(vi) . . . the flying, unending, smoke-coloured snow . . .
(vii) . . . to the close and holy darkness

5. Which word best describes the author's attitude?

depressed indifferent excited nostalgic mysterious

5 Christmas miscellany

A traditional English Christmas Carol

THE HOLLY AND THE IVY

The holly and the ivy
  When they are both full grown,
Of all the trees that are in the wood,
  The holly bears the crown.
(Chorus)
The rising of the sun
  And the running of the deer,
The playing of the merry organ,
  Sweet singing in the choir:

Christmas Pudding

INGREDIENTS

225g (8 oz) flour
110g (4 oz) fresh, white breadcrumbs
225g (8 oz) Barbados sugar
6 eggs
225g (8 oz) currants
338g (12 oz) sultanas
338g (12 oz) raisins
112g (4 oz) candied peel
150ml (¼ pint) brown ale
2 x 15ml spoons (2 tablespoons) brandy
175g (6 oz) blanched, slivered almonds
225g (8 oz) suet
110g (4 oz) glacé cherries
1 cooking apple
grated rind of large lemon
grated rind and juice of 2 oranges
1 x 5ml spoon (1 teaspoon) mixed spice
½ x 5ml spoon (½ teaspoon) cinnamon
½ grated nutmeg
1 x 5ml spoon (1 teaspoon) salt

METHOD

Finely chop the cherries and the candied peel, put them in a large, deep bowl with the rest of the dried fruit. Peel, slice and chop the apple, add the grated lemon and orange peel and the almonds. Now add the suet, flour, breadcrumbs, sugar and spices and the salt. Mix thoroughly, add the well-beaten eggs, the ale and the brandy and the fruit juice. Stir and leave overnight. Put the mixture into pudding basins and leave a few centimetres at the top, for the mixture to swell. Cover with greaseproof paper (or foil), then with a cloth securely tied below the rim with string, put the puddings in pans, each on a trivet if possible, and with water three-quarters of the way up the basins. Simmer on a very low heat for 8 hours, replenishing with boiling water when necessary. The puddings should be left to mature for a month before Christmas. When you are ready to use them, change the cloth on each basin for a fresh one, put the puddings to boil on a low heat as before, and simmer for two hours. Before taking the puddings to table, warm some brandy in a saucepan, pour over the puddings and set light to it with a taper. Serve with brandy-butter or cream. If you are of a mind to do so, wrap some sixpences in paper, and press them into the pudding on the top, before inverting it on to the serving dish.

from *Mrs Bridges' Upstairs and Downstairs Cookery Book*

Sort the ingredients into the following groups, like this:

DRIED FRUITS	FRESH FRUITS	OTHER DRY INGREDIENTS	LIQUIDS	SPICES
currants	apple	flour		

Read the method and find:

– 3 actions which you would do with a *knife*
– 2 actions which you would do with a *spoon*.

What is the difference between 'simmer' and 'boil'?

Are there any traditional dishes associated with Christmas or a similar festival in your country? If so, write down the recipe: list the ingredients and the method of preparing the dish.

6 A Christmas Story

Charles Dickens (1812–70), one of the greatest English novelists, was very influential in creating the traditions connected with the English celebration of Christmas. He did this through his immensely popular Christmas books and stories. One of these, *A Christmas Carol,* published in 1843, has become a Christmas classic. It tells of a mean and miserable old man called Scrooge, who has a series of visions on Christmas Eve. As a result of his dreams, he wakes up on Christmas morning a different man and joins in the festivities that everyone should have at Christmas.

This is how *A Christmas Carol* starts. It is a bitterly cold and foggy Christmas Eve. Everyone is happily getting ready to celebrate Christmas, but Scrooge is in his office counting his money. He hates Christmas. For him it is 'Humbug!'

Listen and read.

nce upon a time – of all the good days in the year, on Christmas Eve – old Scrooge sat busy in his counting-house. It was cold, bleak, biting weather: foggy withal*: and he could hear the people in the court outside, go wheezing up and down, beating their hands upon their breasts, and stamping their feet upon the pavement stones to warm them. The city clocks had only just gone three, but it was quite dark already – it had not been light all day – and candles were flaring in the windows of the neighbouring offices, like ruddy smears upon the palpable brown air. The fog came pouring in at every chink and keyhole, and was so dense without*, that although the court was of the narrowest, the houses opposite were mere phantoms.

The door of Scrooge's counting-house was open that he might keep his eye upon his clerk, who in a dismal little cell beyond, a sort of tank, was copying letters. Scrooge had a very small fire, but the clerk's fire was so very much smaller that it looked like one coal. But he couldn't replenish it, for Scrooge kept the coal-box in his own room; and so surely as the clerk came in with the shovel, the master predicted that it would be necessary for them to part. Wherefore* the clerk put on his white comforter, and tried to warm himself at the candle; in which effort, not being a man of strong imagination, he failed.

'A merry Christmas, uncle! God save you!' cried a cheerful voice. It was the voice of Scrooge's nephew, who came upon him so quickly that this was the first intimation he had of his approach. 'Bah!' said Scrooge, 'Humbug!'*

He had so heated himself with rapid walking in the fog and frost, this nephew of Scrooge's, that he was all in a glow; his face was ruddy and handsome; his eyes sparkled, and his breath smoked again.

'Christmas a humbug, uncle!' said Scrooge's nephew. 'You don't mean that, I am sure?'

'I do,' said Scrooge. 'Merry Christmas! What right have you to be merry? What reason have you to be merry? You're poor enough.'

'Come, then,' returned the nephew gaily. 'What right have you to be dismal? What reason have you to be morose? You're rich enough.'

Scrooge having no better answer ready on the spur of the moment, said, 'Bah!' again; and followed it up with 'Humbug.'

'Don't be cross, uncle!' said the nephew.

'What else can I be,' returned the uncle, 'when I live in such a world of fools as this? Merry Christmas! Out upon* merry Christmas! What's Christmas time to you but a time for paying bills without money; a time for finding yourself a year older, but not an hour richer; a time for balancing your books and having every item in 'em through a round dozen of months presented dead against you? If I could work my will,' said Scrooge indignantly, 'every idiot who goes about with "Merry Christmas" on his lips should be boiled with his own pudding, and buried with a stake of holly through his heart. He should!'

'Uncle!' pleaded the nephew.

'Nephew!' returned the uncle, sternly, 'keep Christmas in your own way, and let me keep it in mine.'

Note: archaic English

withal = too
without = outside
wherefore = and so
humbug = nonsense
out upon = i.e. I don't care about

1. Imagine that you are preparing the scene from A Christmas Carol **as part of a TV production. You are the scriptwriter. Write brief notes describing the scene under the headings below.**

Scene 1: Scrooge's Office

Exterior set: ....

Interior set: ....

Character of Scrooge: ....

Character of Scrooge's nephew:

....

Weather effects: ....

Lighting effects: ....

2. Now put yourself in the position of the actor playing the clerk. Imagine what he might say. Use the questions below to help you. First make notes and then write, like this:

'My name is Bob Cratchit. I am Scrooge's clerk.'

What are you doing at the moment?
What is the room like? Describe it and say what you feel about it.
What do you feel about Scrooge?
What are you thinking as you work?
What are you looking forward to doing?

Now you are the actor playing Scrooge. What might he say?

'My name is Scrooge ...'

What are you doing at the moment?
What is your clerk doing? What do you think of him?
What do you think about Christmas?
What are you thinking of as you work?
What do you think of your nephew?
What are you going to do this evening and tomorrow?

3. In groups of three read the extract from, 'A merry Christmas, uncle!' to the end of the passage: one person reads as the narrator, the other as Scrooge and the other as the nephew.

7 Writing

Describe a festival or celebration that is held in your country. Give your own opinion of it. Make notes following the pattern below. Add further 'branches' and notes as you wish. Notice any topics you have not talked about. Add any of your own.

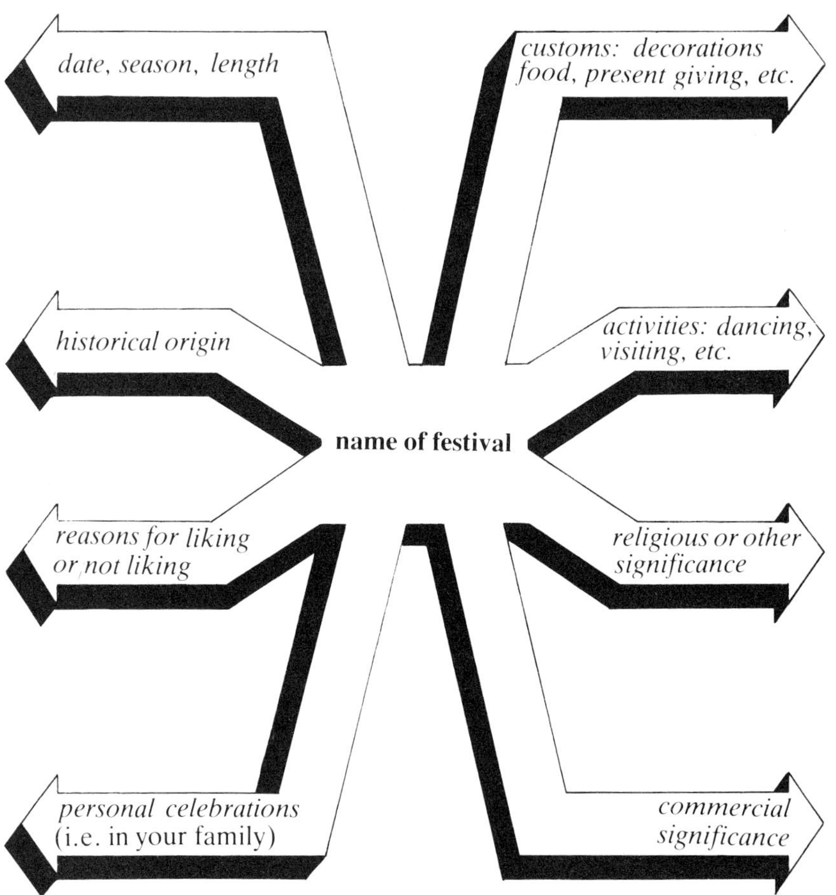

Use the guide below when you write your composition.

PARAGRAPH 1	**Introduction** Name of festival/country; season and length
PARAGRAPH 2	**Main contents (1)** Historical/religious or other significance
PARAGRAPH 3	**Main contents (2)** Preparations; customs; activities
PARAGRAPH 4	**Main contents (3)** Personal celebrations
PARAGRAPH 5	**Conclusion** Commercial significance Personal views about festival

Oral exercises

1. Defining by category

What's a float?
As far as I know, it's some sort of lorry.

1 mistletoe 3 mince-pie 5 port
2 parsnip 4 holly 6 Mardi Gras

Choose from these categories:
festival tree drink plant
vegetable cake or pudding

2. Recalling memories (1)

Two people are recalling memories of their childhood.

I used to sleep in my parents' room.
Yes, I remember sleeping in my parents' room as a child, too.

1. We used to go to circuses.
2. I collected stamps.
3. And I spent most of my pocket money on comics.
4. I used to listen to the radio a lot.
5. I remember I used to read fairy tales.

3. Recalling memories (2)

Did you use to get into trouble a lot?
I didn't, but I remember my brother getting into trouble a lot.

1. Did you belong to a secret club when you were a child?
2. Were you frightened of the dark?
3. Were you clever at school?
4. Did you ever buy pop records?
5. Did you ever learn to play the piano?

4. Talking about festivities and celebrations
(Open exercise)

Think of a festival and answer these questions about it.

What happens the day before?
The day before, (everyone decorates the Christmas tree)

Repeat the time phrase each time you answer.

1. What happens in the morning?
2. What happens in the afternoon?
3. What happens in the evening?
4. What happens on the day after?
5. What happens at the end of the festive period?

Unit 9 Study focus

Interaction

FUNCTION	STRUCTURE
1. Defining terms	present and past participles e.g. 'a cake containing . . .,' 'a festival held . . .'
2. Recalling memories	'remember' + verb (ing) 'remember somebody' + verb (ing)
3. Asking and talking about festivals and traditions	present simple active and passive distributive pronouns ('each', 'every') quantifiers ('both', 'all' etc.)
4. Describing order of events	time phrases and clauses e.g. 'on the morning of . . .', 'as soon as . . .'

Vocabulary

Traditions and festivities
Christmas
Food: preparation and cooking

Writing skills

1. Note-taking under headings from a text
2. Dictionary definitions
3. Listing ingredients
4. Writing recipes (instructions for cooking)
5. Guided composition about a festival (descriptive)

Unit 10 Consolidation

1

The story of Romeo and Juliet was used as the basis for an American musical about rival gangs in New York.

Romeo and Juliet

This is one of Shakespeare's earliest plays, written at the same time as the *Sonnets* and *A Midsummer Night's Dream,* sometime around 1595.

THE PLOT

In Verona the ancient feud between two families, the Capulets and Montagues, breaks out again and even the Prince is unable to pacify them.

Romeo, the son of Montague, and his friends Benvolio and Mercutio, attend a masked ball in the Capulet household. There he sees Juliet and instantly falls in love with her. While trying to lose his friends, Romeo finds himself at Juliet's balcony and overhears her declaring her love for him, which he returns. The next day, with the help of her nurse and Romeo's confessor, Friar Lawrence, they are secretly married.

Romeo is challenged to a duel by Juliet's cousin, Tybalt. He refuses to fight but Mercutio takes his place and is killed. Romeo avenges his friend's death by killing Tybalt. The Prince banishes him from Verona and, after secretly spending his wedding night with Juliet, he flees to Mantua.

Juliet's father arranges for her to be married to Paris, a kinsman of the Prince. In desperation she seeks help from Friar Lawrence, who gives her a sleeping potion that will make her appear dead. Romeo is to be reunited with her after she has been 'buried'. He writes to Romeo of the plan but the message miscarries. Romeo hears that Juliet is dead and buys poison, resolving to die by her side.

With Juliet's apparently dead body in his arms, Romeo takes the poison. A moment later Juliet awakens and seeing that Romeo is dead, she too kills herself. Over the bodies of their two dead children, the Capulets and Montagues are reconciled.

1. Find the words in the text about Romeo and Juliet **which mean approximately the same as:**

- a quarrel
- a dance
- punishes someone for something
- sends away as a punishment
- runs away
- a relative
- a drink which has a hypnotic effect
- is not received
- resolve their arguments and make peace.

2. Rewrite or retell the story of Romeo and Juliet **in the** past tense, **like this:**

'In Verona the ancient feud ...... broke out again and ......

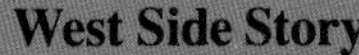

West Side Story

The Jets
Riff – leader, Tony – Riff's friend

The Sharks
Bernardo – leader, Chino – Maria's fiancé, Maria – Bernardo's sister, Anita – Bernardo's girl friend

New York/street feud/gangs/Jets, led by Riff, vs Sharks, led by Bernardo

Tony/friend of Riff/dances on Sharks' territory/meets Maria/love

Tony on fire-escape outside Maria's flat/declare love for each other

Jets challenge Sharks to a 'rumble'/Riff killed by Bernardo/Tony kills Bernardo/hides in candy store/ Chino after him with gun

Maria wants to join Tony/Anita heartbroken over Bernardo's death but agrees to take message from Maria to Tony/attacked by Jets in candy store/in revenge gives different message: Chino has killed Maria because love for Tony/Tony hears message/goes to streets to find Chino/wants to be killed

Suddenly sees Maria/runs to her/too late/shot by Chino/ Maria weeps over body of Tony/Jets and Sharks reconciled over funeral.

3. Look at the pictures and the list of characters above. Use these and the notes to say what happens in West Side Story. **Use the same paragraph division as for** Romeo and Juliet.

4. Discuss the similarities and the differences between the two stories. Use these phrases:

In both *Romeo and Juliet* and *West Side Story,* . . .
In *Romeo and Juliet* . . ., whereas in *West Side Story* . . .
In *Romeo and Juliet* . . . . In *West Side Story,* on the other hand, . . .

5. Write or tell the plot of a story of love and/or tragedy you have seen or read.

2

Your Questions Answered

BY DOCTOR MARY DAWSON

Backache

Q. Recently, I was struck down with acute backache. My doctor told me to rest in bed for two weeks. He also prescribed painkillers for me that were so strong I hardly knew what I was doing. Then I had an X-ray which revealed that I had a prolapsed disc. What does this mean exactly and how long will it be before I'm better?

Mrs A

A. A prolapsed disc, commonly called a slipped disc, is, more often than not, quite serious. To start with the pain is very acute, and bed rest and painkilling drugs are always given as part of the treatment. The pain is not restricted to the back and often runs down the sciatic nerve and causes pains in the legs. The pain is often made worse when the patient coughs, sneezes or laughs. After a period of time, people with prolapsed discs often experience a feeling of pins and needles, or numbness in the feet and legs.

You may feel that the future doesn't look very bright and I must advise you not to be too optimistic about making a *complete* recovery. In many cases, a prolapsed disc settles down with time, but I think you should be prepared for your condition to continue for some time. This means a great deal of patience on your part. I am sorry that I cannot be more positive, but don't lose heart!

Bleeding gums

Q. I have an awful problem. For several weeks, my gums have been sore and red and eating has been painful. My gums bleed if I touch them, so you can imagine how painful it is to eat a meal. I know I ought to see the dentist, but I'm terrified at the thought. I haven't seen a dentist for 20 years.

Mrs B

A. That's why you have this inflammation of the gums! It's called gingivitis and is often due to the build-up of tartar on the teeth. Tartar is a substance the dentist removes when you have a check-up. Good oral hygiene – which includes regular dental care – is essential for healthy gums. Untreated gingivitis can lead eventually to loss of all the teeth.

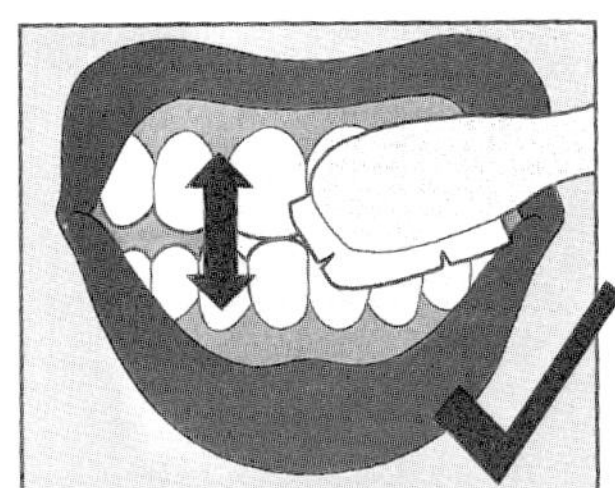

how to brush your teeth

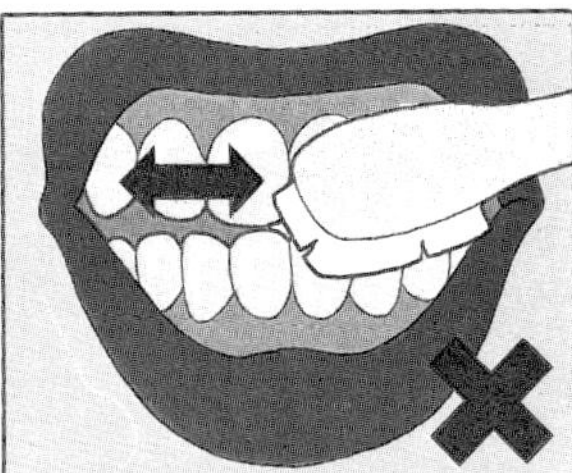

how not *to brush your teeth*

1. Read both letters. In each case note down:

	LETTER 1	LETTER 2
The symptoms		
The diagnosis		
The treatment		

2. Complete this conversation between Mrs A and her doctor when she first went to see him.

DR: Now what seems ....?
MRS A: I've ...... awful pain in ...... and in ......, doctor.
DR: Let me have a .... Mm. I'm afraid you've ...... a ....
MRS A: Oh really? What ...... do then?
DR: If ...... you, I ...... straight to bed and stay there .... I'll give you some ...... too, but I'm afraid it ...... time to get better. You'll have to ......
MRS A: I see. Is there ...... I ...... do?
DR: No, not really. But I must warn you, every time you ...... or ...... or ...... it'll hurt. You'll just have to expect that. Also your leg and ...... may feel ...... Rather like pins and needles.

3. Roleplay the conversation between Mrs A and her employer when she telephones him to say that she cannot come in to work.

4. Writing

Write a letter to Doctor Mary Dawson and describe the symptoms for insomnia or any disability that you are familiar with. Then write Dr Dawson's reply, giving a diagnosis and suggesting a course of action.

WELCOME TO

Trade Winds Hotel

ADVICE TO GUESTS

Valuables

Please place these in the hotel safe. The management cannot accept responsibility for the loss of articles or money from the hotel rooms.
You are advised not to take money or valuables on the beach.

Accounts

Kindly settle all your accounts the evening before your departure. Private cheques may only be accepted by prior arrangement with the cashier.

Rooms

To be vacated by 10.30 am on the day of departure please.

Monkeys

Please do not feed the monkeys. They can be dangerous.

Palm Trees

Beware of falling coconuts. The hotel cannot be held responsible for falling objects from trees.

Coral reef

The reef is protected and shells may only be collected by licence holders.

Sun

The sun's rays are very powerful, even on cloudy days. Please be careful.

Telephone

The switchboard is closed from midnight until 7 am except for emergencies.

Use the notice above to make statements like this:

You're supposed to . . .
not supposed to . . .

or You're not allowed to . . .
or You should/shouldn't . . .

❹ The search for the Northwest Passage

Before you read, find on the map:

the Arctic Ocean, the Pacific Ocean, the Coast Range, the Great Slave Lake, and the Peace, Mackenzie and Bella Coola rivers.

MACKENZIE, Sir ALEXANDER (c.1755–1820) Scottish-born Canadian explorer, who is thought to be the first person to cross the whole breadth of North America from east to west. He explored the then unknown northwest of the North American continent. In 1789, after several years working in the fur trade, Mackenzie started his first journey of exploration with the intention of reaching the Pacific Ocean. Travelling up to the Great Slave Lake, he continued west and then north for 1,600 km (1,000 miles). Instead of reaching the Pacific he reached the Arctic Ocean. Three years later, Mackenzie set out with a party of British and French settlers and American Indians in the hope of reaching the Pacific. They travelled west along the Peace River and travelled over 800 km (500 miles) to its source. In spite of an accident in which they lost most of their provisions, they managed to cross the high and rugged Coast Range and, in canoes, they travelled down the Bella Coola River. Mackenzie and his party reached the Pacific coast near Cape Menzies in 1793. After living in Canada for some years, Mackenzie returned to Scotland, where he died in 1820.

> *Having worked* for several years in the fur trade, *Mackenzie started* his first journey of exploration.

Using the text as a source of information, complete the following sentences in the same way:

1. . . . . . . the Great Slave Lake, he . . . .
2. . . . . . . the Peace River, they . . . .
3. . . . . . . nearly all their provisions, they nevertheless . . . .
4. . . . . . . the Coast Range, they . . . .
5. . . . . . . in Canada for several years, Mackenzie . . .

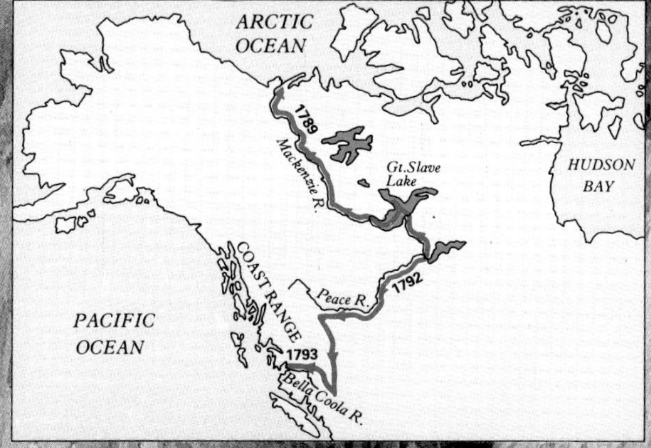

The following passage is based on an account of Mackenzie's first exploration

Alexander Mackenzie was the first man to travel across the continent of North America all the way from the east coast to the west coast. He had set out to find a sea route which would link the Atlantic Ocean with the Pacific. The route was to be called the Northwest Passage.

Having been brought up in the remote northernmost part of Scotland's Western Isles, Mackenzie had experienced the hardships which can be caused by extreme cold. He added to this experience by working as a young man for the Hudson's Bay Company in North America. This company, which was founded in 1670, had an almost complete monopoly of the rich fur trade in the Northwest Territories. Mackenzie worked for several years at the company's lonely trading outpost on the shores of Lake Athabaska, where he learned everything he could from the older fur trappers about the cold and hostile wilderness of the Northwest Territories.

On 3rd June 1789, he set out on his first journey of exploration. He was then 34 years old. With him he took a team of five trappers in one large birch-bark canoe with sails, and in another five Indians, including one who acted as a guide and as an interpreter. Driving his party hard, Mackenzie travelled 58 kilometres (36 miles) on the first day and 130 km (81 miles) on the second. Soon they reached the Great Slave Lake which, even at this time of year, was covered with broken ice. The canoes were in constant danger of being crushed. Not only this, but the party were tormented by plagues of mosquitoes. They sailed towards the west looking for an exit from the lake.

Eventually, they found a river, which now bears Mackenzie's name. The current was strong and, with a good wind behind them, they raised the sails on their canoes and travelled 480 kilometres (300 miles) along the river towards the west. Then, suddenly, they saw the Rocky Mountains in front of them, and the river went north.

Still optimistic of reaching the Pacific, Mackenzie continued to follow the river, in spite of being told by the Indians they met along its banks that it would probably take a lifetime to reach its source.

He soon realised, when he took his bearings, that he had come so far north that they were only one degree from the Arctic Circle. The river they were following would not end in the Pacific but in the Arctic Ocean. Nevertheless, he urged the party on and in time reached the northern ocean.

Winter was now approaching so it was essential to turn back to avoid it. Mackenzie and his men reached home three months after the start of their journey. They had covered 4,800 km (3,000 miles) but they had not reached the Pacific.

Realising that he was not as well prepared as he should be, either materially or psychologically, Mackenzie returned to Britain to get ready for his next journey. At home he began to assemble a collection of instruments and equipment. He also increased his knowledge of geography and of the techniques of surveying. Feeling better equipped and more confident, he returned to his fur trader's post ready for another attempt to find the Northwest Passage.

Word study

(i) Put the following words in alphabetical order:
exploration essential experience extreme eventually

(ii) Complete the following statements:
Hostile must mean something like ....
Birch must be a kind of ....
A *canoe* must be a kind of ....
A *mosquito* must be a kind of ....
A *plague* must here mean something like ......
Surveying must mean something like ....

(iii) Look up the following three words in a monolingual dictionary. Select and write down the appropriate meaning for each in this context:

experience current party

(iv) Fill in the missing adjective or adverb form in the following list:

extreme	
	materially
	mentally
essential	
remote	
confident	

Make sentences using the other form of the word.

(v) Mark where the main stress falls in these words:
surveying materially mosquitoes
interpreter monopoly increased

1. Which of the following statements are true and which are false? Correct those which are false.

Mackenzie learnt all he knew about exploring from his early life in the Western Isles of Scotland.
Mackenzie's party covered over 160 km (100 miles) in the first two days.
It was winter when they reached the Great Slave Lake.
The river turned north after 480km (300 miles).
Mackenzie took three months to reach the Pacific Ocean.
Mackenzie felt himself to be perfectly well trained and equipped for his expedition.

2. Choose two examples from the text to support the following statements about Mackenzie.

Mackenzie had experienced extremes of cold.
The journey along the Great Slave Lake was hazardous and unpleasant.
The journey west out of the lake was easier.
Mackenzie was a strong-willed and determined man.
Mackenzie prepared himself seriously for his second expedition.

Connect all the topic sentences with their examples, like this:

Mackenzie had experienced extremes of cold. For example/instance, ...
Furthermore/Moreover, ...

Sir Alexander Mackenzie

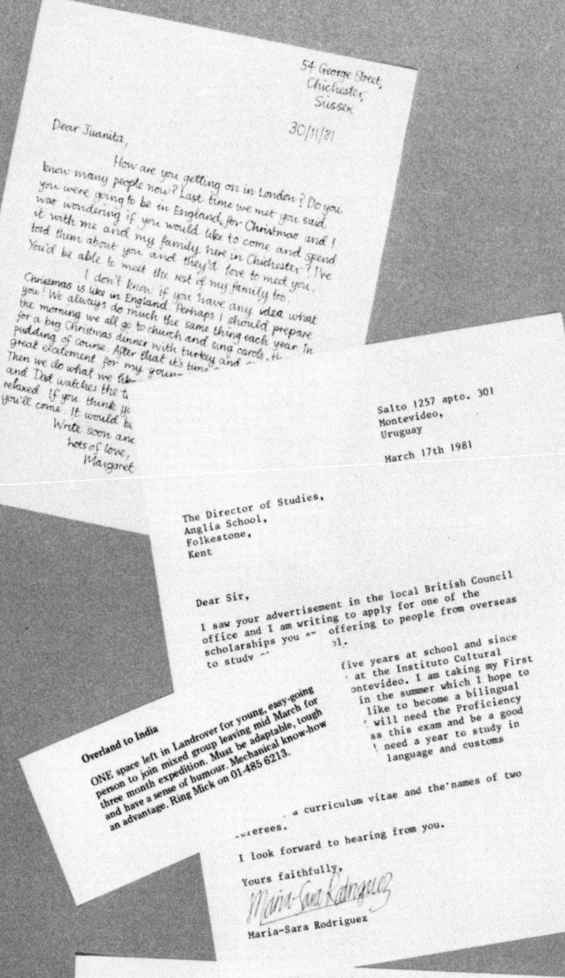

54 George Street,
Chichester,
Sussex

30/11/81

Dear Juanita,

How are you getting on in London? Do you know many people now? Last time we met you said you were going to be in England for Christmas and I was wondering if you would like to come and spend it with me and my family here in Chichester? I've told them about you and they'd love to meet you. You'd be able to meet the rest of my family too.

I don't know if you have any idea what Christmas is like in England. Perhaps I should prepare you! We always do much the same thing each year. In the morning we all go to church and sing carols, [illegible] for a big Christmas dinner with turkey and [illegible] pudding of course. After that it's time [illegible] great excitement for my young[illegible] Then we do what we [illegible] and Dad watches the t[illegible] relaxed. If you think y[illegible] you'll come. It would b[illegible]

Write soon and [illegible]

Lots of love,

Margaret

Salto 1257 apto. 301
Montevideo,
Uruguay

March 17th 1981

The Director of Studies,
Anglia School,
Folkestone,
Kent

Dear Sir,

I saw your advertisement in the local British Council office and I am writing to apply for one of the scholarships you are offering to people from overseas to study [illegible]ol.

[illegible] five years at school and since [illegible] at the Instituto Cultural [illegible]ontevideo. I am taking my First [illegible] in the summer which I hope to [illegible] like to become a bilingual [illegible] will need the Proficiency [illegible] as this exam and be a good [illegible] need a year to study in [illegible] language and customs

[illegible] a curriculum vitae and the names of two [illegible]referees.

I look forward to hearing from you.

Yours faithfully,

Maria-Sara Rodriguez

Overland to India

ONE space left in Landrover for young, easy-going person to join mixed group leaving mid March for three month expedition. Must be adaptable, tough and have a sense of humour. Mechanical know-how an advantage. Ring Mick on 01-485 6213.

Helen: Have you seen Kramer versus Kramer?
Pete: Yes, I have. I saw it on Saturday actually.
Helen: What did you think of it?
Pete: I thought it was very good. Didn't you?
Helen: I'm not sure. I liked parts of it but it was a bit too sentimental for my taste.
Pete: Really? I thought the boy acted superbly and Dustin Hoffman was marvellous as the father.
Helen: Yes, it wasn't too bad. It was beautifully photographed anyway. But, to be honest, that sort of film doesn't do much for me. I prefer less sentimental films.

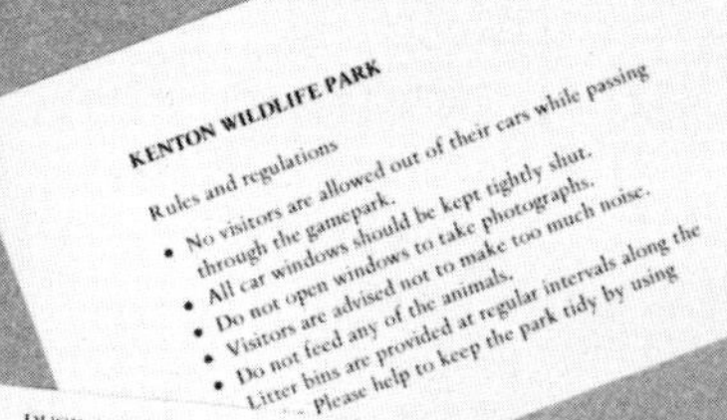

KENTON WILDLIFE PARK

Rules and regulations

- No visitors are allowed out of their cars while passing through the gamepark.
- All car windows should be kept tightly shut.
- Do not open windows to take photographs.
- Visitors are advised not to make too much noise.
- Do not feed any of the animals.
- Litter bins are provided at regular intervals along the [illegible] Please help to keep the park tidy by using [illegible]

HALLOWEEN GAMES: DUCK APPLE

Fill a large bowl with cold (sometimes soapy) water and float a number of apples in it. One or two players at a time get down on their knees and, with their hands behind their backs, try to get hold of one of the apples with their teeth. If they manage to do it, they may eat the apple.

Writing tasks

1. *An informal letter*

Write a letter to a foreign friend, inviting him/her to spend Christmas or a similar festive day, with you. Explain what you are planning to do and how you will spend the day(s).

2. *A formal letter*

Write a letter to the head of a school/college/university in Britain explaining that you want to apply for one of the scholarships they are offering to people from overseas. Say why you think you qualify for a scholarship and why you think you would benefit from a period of study in Britain.

3. *An advertisement*

Write an advertisement for someone to join your mixed party of young people who are intending to go on an expedition to India or Africa in the spring. Mention the qualities you think will be necessary for anyone joining your expedition.

4. *A conversation*

Write a conversation between yourself and a friend about a film you have both seen. Agree and disagree about different aspects of its production.

5. *A list*

Write a list of rules and regulations for a Nature Reserve or Wild Life Park.

6. *Instructions*

Describe how you:
either make a simple table decoration *or* prepare a festive dish *or* treat somebody for a burn or for fainting *or* play a game associated with a festival in your country.

7. *A composition*

Write a short composition about an exciting or important day in your life. Start your composition like this:
One of the most . . . days in my life was the day I . . .

Unit 11 Mind over matter

Before you start:

Do you think many people suffer from being depressed?

Do you think you need to go to specialists to learn more about yourself and change your life patterns?

Do you think dreams reflect what goes on in everyday life?

❶ Are you assertive enough in today's difficult world?

1 Do you buy things you don't really want because it is difficult to say 'No' to the salesperson?

2 Do you hesitate to return items to a shop even when there is good reason to do so?

3 If someone talks in a loud voice during a film, play or concert, can you ask him/her to be quiet?

4 Can you begin a conversation with a stranger?

5 When a friend makes an unreasonable request, are you able to refuse?

6 Can you ask favours or make requests of your friends?

7 Can you criticise a friend?

8 Can you praise a friend?

9 When someone compliments you, do you know what to say?

10 Do people tend to exploit you or push you around?

1. Note down your own answers to the questions. Mark the answers which show that you are unassertive.

2. With a partner, work out what you would say:

- to some people who started whispering in a concert
- to a friend who asked you to lend him/her £20
- to a stranger in a bus queue after waiting for ten minutes
- to a friend who lets her child stay up till very late every evening
- to a friend who has just got a job he/she has always wanted
- to a friend who says 'I like you in that colour, it suits you.'
- to your boss who asks you to stay late and do some work for him/her for the fourth time in one week.

Examples:
Would you mind . . .ing . . .?
Do you think you could . . .?
I'm sorry, but I'm afraid . . .

❷ Assertiveness training

The world contains many people who don't recognise their own strengths or who have learnt to act in inferior ways because they believe themselves to be inferior. They find it impossible to express emotions like anger or tenderness. They follow the wishes of others and hold their own desires inside themselves. Because they have no control of their own lives, they

become increasingly unsure. They become 'unassertive'. Often a victim of unassertiveness does not recognise it as an emotional problem. From passivity and fear, he or she justifies it with excuses: 'If I answer him back, he'll be angry with me'. . .'Unless I do what she wants, she'll leave me'. . . 'Why bother to try? I'm bound to fail'. This is the sort of behaviour you learn, and you can unlearn it. You can find the answers to your problems in a new scientific technique called Assertiveness Training (AT), through which, by changing your actions, you change your attitudes and feelings towards yourself. Just as you have trained yourself to be neurotic, you can teach yourself to be normal.

from an article on Attitude Training

Word study

(i) Find all the words in the text which have a negative meaning, e.g. 'inferior'.

(ii) Use a dictionary to find the corresponding adjective or noun for the following words:

NOUN	ADJECTIVE	NOUN	ADJECTIVE
strength	strong	tenderness	....
....	inferior	passivity	....
emotion	....	fear	....
anger	....	....	neurotic

1.

Unless I do what she wants, she'll leave me.

Look at the examples of excuses in the text. Try to think of two more on the same pattern:

'If I ...., he/she will/won't ....'
'Unless I ...., he/she will/won't ....'

2. Complete this summary of the text:

The authors are trying to present a new technique called .... which is designed to help people who .... inferior. These sorts of people find it difficult to ..... They also tend to ..... The sort of things they say as an excuse are: 'If ....'

❸ Case study

Sally Jones lived in a state of constant upset, feeling she was always the scapegoat when things went wrong. One day she returned to her office after a solitary lunch ('People always pick on me, so it's easier to be by myself.') and the business manager yelled at her, 'You left the xerox room in an awful mess.' He accused her unfairly, misled by wrong information.

Sally was about to answer defensively with 'I wasn't in the xerox room today,' but just in time remembered her AT. She told her boss, 'Now *you* just apologise.' Startled by her change in manner, the boss shot back, 'Apologise for what?' Said Sally firmly, 'For yelling at me for something I didn't do.'

She got her apology and realised that, having answered one accusation assertively, she could do this on other occasions – and did. As a result of being assertive, not only did she find that her relations on the job changed, but she began lunching with people and making friends.

Check

Why did Sally always have lunch on her own?
What did the manager accuse Sally of doing?
Why was this unfair?
What was wrong with the response that Sally started to make – 'I wasn't in the xerox room'?
What would have been a better response?

In your own words, say why the manager was startled.
What happened after this incident?

1.

> 'You left the xerox room in an awful mess.'
> He accused her of leaving the xerox room in an awful mess.

Report the following accusations in the same way:

'You always have lunch by yourself!'
'You don't get on well with the other staff!'
'You always forget to switch off the lights!'
'You make spelling mistakes in letters!'
'You never lock the stock cupboard!'

2.

> Sally disliked her job and found it difficult to get on with her boss.
>
> *Not only* did Sally dislike her job, *but* she found it difficult to get on with her boss.
>
> *Not only* did Sally dislike her job, she *also* found it difficult to get on with her boss.

Change the sentences below in the same way:

Sally often felt inadequate and saw herself as the scapegoat.
She started to answer assertively and told people to apologise.
She looked more cheerful and said what she thought.
She applied for another job and moved to a new flat.
She enjoyed her new job and got an increase in pay.

❹ Coping with moods

Depression:

Whenever / If ever	I feel depressed, I have a hot bath.

Once I've	soaked in it . . . / done that . . .	for a few minutes, I'm all right again.

How do you cope with the following moods?

anger	depression	tiredness	boredom
guilt	loneliness	fear	

Choose suitable 'cures' from this list:

go to bed	throw things at the wall
have something to eat	have a hot bath
go to the library	have a drink
shut myself in my room	put my best clothes on and go out
telephone a good friend	put my feet up and watch television
go to the cinema	go out and buy myself something

Make sentences like this:

Whenever / If ever	I feel . . ., I . . . Once I've . . ., I'm all right.

Suggest your own personal 'cures' if you like.

❺ Sigmund Freud (1856-1939)

Sigmund Freud was born in Moravia but moved to Vienna with his parents at the age of four. He is known as the inventor of psychoanalysis, that is to say, a method of treating people with mental or nervous illnesses. During treatment the patient is made to examine everything he can remember about his past life – often going back to childhood – which may have caused the illness. Freud's theory was that these past experiences have been repressed, or held back, in the unconscious mind.

One way of explaining the concept of the conscious and the un-, or subconscious mind, is to think of an iceberg, one tenth of which is visible on the surface of the sea, but the remaining nine-tenths of which lie hidden in the deep, dark waters.

By bringing the sublimated experiences to the surface and out into the conscious mind, the patient and therapist can analyse all the different parts which make up the present psychological situation. In other words, they analyse or examine any anxiety complexes, phobias or obsessions that the patient may have. This deep analysis of past experiences, Freud believed, would help to cure the patient.

Freud's major work is called *The Interpretation of Dreams*, a book which has had a revolutionary influence on 20th century ideas. In it Freud expresses the theory that the unconscious mind tries to reach consciousness during sleep, through the process of dreaming. Through symbols and images, almost like a film, dreams realise or give vent to our unconscious fears and desires. Freud believed that the analysis of dreams could help us to understand our waking lives.

1. Notice these different ways of defining the meaning of words and ideas in the text:

(i) '. . . that these past experiences have been repressed, *or* held back, . . .' (line 9)
'or' means 'or in other words' in this sense and is generally used with synonyms.

(ii) '. . .psychoanalysis, *that is to say*, a method of treating people . . .. (line 3)
'that is to say' is generally used with longer explanations and can occur mid-sentence. In making notes, it is abbreviated to 'i.e.'

(iii) '. . .make up the present psychological situation. *In other words*, they analyse . . .' (lines 19 and 20)
'In other words' is generally used to rephrase an idea. It is usually placed at the beginning of a sentence.

2. Using the words and phrases in Exercise 1 join the two parts of the following sentences to make definitions.

These experiences have been repressed/hidden under the surface.
The patient and the therapist/specialist can analyse all the different parts.
In most cases they would examine any anxiety complexes, phobias/strong and unnatural fears or dislikes, that the patient may have.
Freud's book had a revolutionary influence on 20th century ideas/most ideas since then show Freud's influence in some way.
Freud believed that the analysis/interpretation of dreams can help us to understand our waking lives.

❻ Noises in the night

People like ghosts. Collections of ghost stories crowd on to our bookshelves; newspaper editors snap up stories of haunted supermarkets or suburban bungalows; and our televisions show ghosts as the leading characters.

People in Anglesey have heard the voice of a dead opera singer near where the singer's house once stood; and the ghostly chanting of monks has been heard emanating from the ruins of an abbey near Beaulieu, one of Britain's stateliest homes.

As old houses settle over the years, the creaks and bumps from their woodwork may have given rise to many minor legends of audible poltergeists. But some such cases, generally termed 'knocking' or 'rapping' poltergeists, seem too elaborate to be so easily explained, like the thumping noises in a small village in Wales, which came (at night) from the shop of a man who was both carpenter and undertaker – and which always presaged a death in the village.

Some invisible ghosts do not find it necessary to work out rapping codes, for they have voices and use them readily. Often the voice merely screams – like the weird cry from an empty field near a house in Sussex, in 1964. The chilling sound lasted fifteen minutes – and the man who heard it later learned that on the same night his father had died, miles away.

A well-known folklorist, named Thomas Westropp, wrote an account, in 1910, of a wildly haunted house in County Clare – full of footsteps and door slamming, but also of eerie whispers, sobbing, muttering, shrieks, and wild laughter. The so-called 'Bell Witch' seems to have been an equally demonic poltergeist, in its relentless haunting of John Bell, a 19th-century Tennessee farmer. (The word 'poltergeist' had not then been adopted into the language; 'witch', then as now, was a handy label.) The symptoms began mildly, with strange scratching noises, snatching of bedclothes, and the like. But soon Bell was suffering torments – not the least of which was the spirit's announcement, in a clear feminine voice, that she intended to make Bell suffer and eventually kill him. But she failed to say why.

In the end, his house echoing with the screeching laughter and derisive comments of the murderous poltergeist, John Bell duly lay down and died. Controversy still rages over how much of the story is exaggeration, how much fraud, how much, if any, reliable.

from *Return from the Dead* by Douglas Hill

Check

What was heard in:
Anglesey?
the ruins of an abbey near Beaulieu?
a small village in Wales?
an empty field near a house in Sussex?
a haunted house in County Clare?
John Bell's farmhouse in Tennessee?

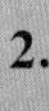

1. Make a list of all the words in the text which are to do with noise. Sort them into these two columns, like this:

ANIMATE WORDS/SOUNDS	INANIMATE WORDS/SOUNDS
chanting	ringing
scream	creak
. . . . . .	. . . . . .
. . . . . .	. . . . . .

2.

I *heard* someone sing*ing*.
I *saw* something mov*ing*.
I *felt* something crawl*ing* over my hand.

Imagine that you spent last night in a large empty house. Strange things happened during the night. Tell your partner what you heard, saw and felt. Use these words to give you some ideas:

run	laugh	brush against
wave	knock	touch
slam	move	

Example:

I saw someone running across the garden into some bushes.

3.

She wanted to *make* him *suffer.*
She did not *let* him *leave* the room.

Look at the following sentences. Express the same meaning using make **or** let **where suitable, like this:**

Goodness! I really jumped when I heard you.
Goodness! You made me jump!

No-one is allowed to come into my room.
My hair stood on end when I heard that knocking sound.
The attic is dangerous. Your children shouldn't go up there.
The picture fell down because of the strong wind.
You mustn't allow the cat to sleep on the beds.

4. Retell the story of the 'Bell Witch' by filling in the missing words in the following text:

The so-called 'Bell Witch' was actually . . . . . which . . . . . a farmer from Tennessee. It started by . . . . . but soon John Bell heard a . . . . . voice which said that she . . . . . and eventually . . . . . Finally, John Bell . . . . . People are still arguing over . . . . . of the story is . . . . .

5. Some friends of yours have asked you to look after their house for the evening while they are away. It is a dark, windy night, and the house is very large and eerie. After an hour you telephone another of your friends to ask him/her to come over and keep you company. Act out or write the telephone conversation between you and your friend. Use these guidelines:

YOU: *Greet friend and say who you are.*
FRIEND: *Greet.*
YOU: *Say where you are and why.*
FRIEND: *Ask what the matter is.*
YOU: *Explain. Say that you are frightened. Ask friend to come over.*
FRIEND: *Ask for further details.*
YOU: *Reply: say what noises you can hear.*
FRIEND: *Agree to come over at once.*
YOU: *Thank and say goodbye.*

7 Listening

Read the case study. Then listen to the tape and suggest which dream Irma had. Explain your reasons, i.e. give an interpretation of the dream.

Irma is a 35 year-old married woman with three children. Once the children were all at school, she went to work in the office of a fashion magazine. She was so efficient and successful that she was made editor. She loves the work, and is now earning more than her husband. He occasionally accuses her of neglecting him and the children and of caring more about the luxuries that her income provides than about the basic happiness of the family unit. She always denies this, feeling that she is successfully balancing her career with her role as wife and mother. However, her husband's sarcastic remarks hurt her deeply.

Writing

Either write a short account of a dream you remember vividly
or write a short account of a supernatural event that has happened to you or a friend.

Oral exercises

1. Stating conditions

A father is explaining to his child the consequences of not doing certain things.

CHILD: I don't want to go to bed now! It's not that late! (fall asleep)
FATHER: *Listen! You'll fall asleep unless you go to bed now.*

1. I don't want to go to bed now. It's not that late. (get tired)
2. Must I have a plaster on this cut? It hurts. (get an infection)
3. No, no, I don't want to put on any sun cream. I don't like it. (get sunburnt)
4. I like the snow. I don't want a hat! (get earache)
5. I can't be bothered to brush my teeth. (get toothache and bad teeth)

2. Listing jobs

Peter is very busy before the summer holidays. He talks to his friend Sharon.

SHARON: Well, you are having a busy time!
PETER: *I know, as well as renewing my passport, I've got to have a cholera injection.*
SHARON: Is that all?
PETER: *No. As well as having a cholera injection, I've got to spend the weekend looking after my mother.*

Things to do
renew passport / have cholera injection / spend weekend looking after mother / arrange office party / buy some light trousers / buy birthday present for Jane / sort out and pay the bills

3. Talking about future plans

Jack is talking to his neighbour's teenage son.

JACK: What are you going to do when you leave school?
BOY: *Oh, once I've left school, I'll earn some money.*

My plans for the future
(i) leave school (ii) earn some money (iii) start a bookshop (iv) employ one or two staff (v) open a chain of bookshops (vi) travel round the world (vii) sell the business and retire!

4. Hearing things

You and a friend are exploring a large, old deserted house . . .

MAN: Listen!
GIRL: What is it?
MAN: *I can hear someone screaming.*

Now you respond to the things you hear on the tape in the same way.

Unit 11 Study focus

Interaction

FUNCTION	STRUCTURE
1. Requesting and refusing politely	'Would you mind' + verb (ing)? 'Do you think you could' + verb? 'I'm sorry, but I'm afraid . . .'
2. Stating conditions	'If'/'Unless' + present tense 'will'/'won't' (1st conditional)
3. Reporting accusations	'He accused her of' + verb (ing)
4. Linking ideas by addition	'Not only' + inversion 'As well as' + verb (ing)
5. Expressing habitual actions	'Whenever' / 'If ever' } + present tense
6. Expressing a point of time	'Once' + present perfect (completed action)
7. Defining by using other words	'or', 'that is to say', 'in other words'

ADDITIONAL STRUCTURES
Verbs of sensation: see, hear, feel + object + verb (ing)
Verbs: make/let + object + infinitive without 'to'

Vocabulary
Nouns and adjectives of emotion
Verbs related to sound

Writing skills
1. Gap-filling summary
2. Guided dialogue
3. Composition: narration

Unit 12 Wonderful world

'It looks like a splendid jewel suspended in space.'
Neil Armstrong, first man on the moon, July 21 1969

Before you start:

To Neil Armstrong the earth looked bright blue, and he could see the brilliant white of the cloud formations, the dark blue of the oceans and the deep brown of the continents.

Which continent do you live in?
What problems exist, do you think, for this 'wonderful world'?

❶ Sri Lanka

1. Read the article on Sri Lanka and complete the chart below.

Type of country: island Geographical location: Capital city: Size: Climate: Main vegetation:	Landscape: Special geographical features: Transport and communication: Natural resources: Wild life:

2. Discuss the following:

(i) Why do you think Arthur C. Clarke, the famous science fiction writer and author of *2001: A Space Odyssey*, has chosen Sri Lanka as his home?

(ii) You and your partner are both enthusiastic photographers. What four things do you think would make good photographic subjects in Sri Lanka?

Sri Lanka is considered to be one of the most beautiful countries in the world. It is just smaller in area than Scotland. Lying off the south-east coast of India, the island of Sri Lanka is separated from the mainland by the Palk Strait. People who live there sometimes call it by an old name which means 'Golden Island' and, in legend, Sinbad the Sailor is said to have visited it and called it 'Serendip' meaning 'Lucky Find'.

As the island lies not very far north of the equator, the climate of Sri Lanka is said to be tropical. It is hot all the year round and there is very little difference between summer and winter. Moreover, heavy rains fall during the monsoon season, causing the climate to be hot and humid. Consequently, vegetation grows dense and thick, and the jungle is so impenetrable in parts of the island that it is difficult to proceed without cutting a path with a machete.

Although the main centres of population are in the flat, fertile coastal regions, many people live in the mountainous country inland. This area contains mountain peaks, two of which – Adam's Peak and Mount Pedro – are twice as high as any mountain in Britain. But, in spite of the mountains and rough terrain, the communications are good and it is easy to travel around the island by road and rail. There are four airports, the main one being Bandaranaike, situated 34 km (21 miles) north of Colombo, the capital of Sri Lanka.

With its rich natural resources, Sri Lanka has an agricultural economy. Rice is grown for local consumption, whereas rubber, produced in the tropical forests, and tea, harvested on the slopes of the inland hills, are the island's most important exports. Coconuts grow in abundance and the sea is rich with fish, which the people catch in small boats with large, three-cornered sails.

Deep in the forests wild animals abound: elephants, leopards, crocodiles, monkeys, snakes and a strange animal called a Giant Monitor, a kind of lizard over two metres (6 feet) long which has strong claws and can climb trees. There are also many rare birds which are hardly seen anywhere else on earth.

It is with some justification that Sinbad the Sailor referred to Sri Lanka as his 'paradise on earth'.

3.

> Sri Lanka *is considered to be* one of the most beautiful countries in the world.
>
> Sinbad the Sailor *is said to have visited* it.
>
> **Note**
> This is more impersonal and objective than 'Many people consider that . . .' and 'They say that . . .' and suits this style of writing.

Rewrite the following statements in the same way, using a passive.

They say that Iceland has a very pleasant climate.
Many people consider that the cathedral in Florence is one of the most beautiful in the world.
Many think that Sweden has one of the richest economies in the world.
They say that pirates invaded the city in the 16th century and stole all the gold and silver from the churches.

4.

> *Lying off* the south-east coast of India, *the island* of Sri Lanka is separated from the mainland by the Palk Strait. = The island lies off . . . and is separated . . .

Rewrite these sentences using a verb ending in ing.

If you approach the island from the north, you can just see the mountain railway.
The village nestles in the valley and seems to have become part of the surrounding hillside.
As I came by air, I didn't get a chance to see the famous coastline.

5.

> Rubber, *produced* in the tropical forests, and tea, *harvested* . . . . ., are the island's most important exports. = Rubber, which is produced . . . . . and tea, which is harvested . . . . . are the island's . . . . .

Rewrite these sentences omitting the word which **and using the past participle of the verb.**

Tea, which they grow in the famous tea gardens, is harvested for export.
The city, which is surrounded by mountains, must have offered good protection against invaders.
The poor harvest, which was brought on by the summer storms, was only one of the island's economic problems last year.

6.

> Many words in English can be used as either a noun or a verb, such as 'export'. But the stress pattern is often different. Usually, nouns are stressed on the first syllable, e.g. 'export and verbs on the second, e.g. ex'port.

Complete the following box and mark the stress pattern for both noun and verb.

NOUN	VERB	NOUN	VERB
export		object	
	import		permit
increase		record	
	transfer		present

Now find the missing words in these sentences and read them out loud.

Marco Polo . . . . . that there were dangerous men in the mountains.
Our rice crops are so low that we will need to . . . . . some this year.
I'm afraid I . . . . . to his accusations.
I need a new work . . . . .

2

1. Study the list of words below and classify them under the following headings, like this:

> *Area or landscape:* desert
> *Climate:* cold
> *Type of land:* volcanic
> *Natural resources (non-edible):* gold
> *Natural resources (edible):* sugar, crops
> *Natural disasters:* flood

There are six words for each group.

famine	coal	coffee	iron ore
temperate	humid	avalanche	fertile
flat	plain	rocky	tea
hilly	jungle	rubber	mountains
valley	earthquake	arable	dry
rural	lake	tropical	drought
maize	rice	timber	wet
potatoes	hurricane	Mediterranean	oil
forest fire	minerals	fruit	forest

2. Suggest the name of a place which:

- grows coffee
- suffers from famine
- produces oil
- has forests and lakes
- has jungle vegetation
- suffers from drought
- has a temperate climate
- is mountainous
- has arable farmland
- produces iron ore

3. Writing

Notice how some of these words are used in the following paragraph about Britain:

Britain is said to have a *temperate* climate. In the south and parts of the midlands, the land is very *arable* and many different sorts of *crops* are grown. The north can be quite *hilly* and in parts of Scotland and Wales you can find *mountains* and *lakes*. As regards natural resources, Britain produces *coal* in the midlands and in Wales, and has its own *oil* source in the North Sea. Apart from *floods* and the occasional *drought*, Britain is fortunate to escape many of the serious disasters that hit other countries.

Look at the photograph of Bora Bora and the information in the chart. Write a paragraph about Bora Bora similar to the one above, using the information given.

BORA BORA

Climate: tropical
Land: fertile: palmtrees, prickly pears
Natural resources: coconuts, fish, sun and water: ideal for tourism
Danger from natural disasters: hurricanes, tornadoes

Either write a similar paragraph about your own country
or write a longer composition, using the text on Sri Lanka as a guide.

4. Discuss and then write your reasons for preferring to live in one or other of the following:

Switzerland or Sri Lanka
Southern California or Australia
Britain or the USA

Use this guide:

Although ....., I would prefer to live in ..... There are several reasons why. *In the first place,* (mention the climate). *Secondly,* (mention the type of landscape, natural features, etc.). *Thirdly,* (mention way of life/the question of natural disasters and anything else you think is relevant).

3 Listening

Listen to a Senegalese student describing the region where he lives in Africa. Make notes under the topic headings in Number 2, Exercise 1. Write a short paragraph describing the region.

4 Writing

You have been shipwrecked in the South Pacific. You managed to float on a raft with a few of your possessions to a deserted island ...

Describe your first impressions of the island and how you spent your first day: how did you get food and drink, where did you sleep, etc? Start your composition like this:

'I looked around me in wonder. Was I really on a desert island? .....'

End it like this:
'And so I lay down to sleep, exhausted after the long day and wondering what the next day would bring.'

5

The River Thames at Richmond near London. Industrial wastes and sewage destroyed most of the fish in the lower parts of the river.

A view of Los Angeles in the USA, where white people enjoy one of the highest standards of living anywhere in the world. The air is also chronically polluted.

An aerial view of a built-up area of a suburb of London

Soft drinks now have dispensable packaging for our convenience.

Discussion

Look at the pictures and describe what you can see. What is the point of each picture – what is each picture trying to show?

Can you see places like this in your country?
Do you buy drink and food in non-disposable containers?
What do you think are the causes of the types of pollution shown in each of these pictures? What can be done to improve the situation?

Before you read:

Are there any rivers or lakes in your town or city?
Would you consider bathing in them?
What sort of things make water dirty?
Which of the following words have 'good' and clean associations and which have 'bad' and dirty associations?

cool spring filth clear ugly pleasure
repulsive poison rotting

❻ Our changing environment

We are camping on an island in Lake George, near the eastern boundary of New York's Adirondacks. We delight in this lake for many reasons, but chief among them is the cool, clear water, so close that ten steps take us from our sleeping bags to the first swim of the day. We drink the lake water – wherever we are, and this is also a special pleasure.

But the water today is seldom as the explorers found it. Our campsite lake, which we drink from, is exceptional. Today no sensible person would dip a drinking cup into the Potomac River, or the Hudson, or the Ohio, or Lake Michigan. Even a woodland spring cannot be trusted unless it has been tested and certified.

A few of the settlers who floated down the Ohio River went ashore and built homes beside a certain creek that flows into the river from the north. The creek was clear and bubbling then. In time it was used to turn a miller's wheel.

Recently I spent most of a day exploring this creek, but not for pleasure. The mill no longer stands. The settlement has become a city. Factories have displaced cornfields, and tall apartment buildings stand where trees once grew. The creek's banks are raw and ugly, strewn with rotting and rusting debris. Between the riverbanks a thick, repulsive, dark fluid flows sluggishly, carrying rags, paper, and assorted filth.

We Americans like to think of ourselves as the cleanest people on earth. Our television screens are preoccupied with soap; our drinking glasses must sparkle and our bed-sheets must be whiter than white. The gleaming, glass-walled residences that overlook the creek have tiled bathrooms and kitchens of stainless steel. But the drains from those shining places discharge into this malodorous ditch, mixing with the wastes of factories and stores, street washings, and other refuse. Shocking as this creek is, it is not the exception. Pollution of our rivers, streams, lakes, and ponds has become the common condition.

As I worked at my campsite table, a young man came by and asked what I was writing about. To keep it short, I said, 'Air and water pollution.' He nodded, then shrugged.

'So what's there to write about?' he demanded. 'So the rivers are dirty. So we make people keep them clean. What else?'

It can seem just that simple. Pollution is often made to seem like a struggle between the Good Guys and the Bad Guys, the Good Guys seeking stiffer laws to stop the greedy Bad Guys from poisoning the air and fouling the water. Here at this lake, the Good Guys are still ahead. Here they have stopped the Bad Guy's occasional offenses. But an army of policemen could not clean up that horrid creek in Ohio. They could drag every offender into court, and the creek would still run foul. The causes of water pollution, and air pollution too, are deep in the fabric of our urban, industrial society. In truth, there are no Good Guys. We are all offenders.

At our island camp we are far removed from such darkened air and befouled water. The air smells of pine, and the water is clear and blue. The landscape seems unmarked by ax or plow. But the appearance of wilderness is deceptive. Even this clear air and water carry the traces of contamination. Even here, birds and fish have been killed by man's new poisons. Here, and at home, we breathe the air and drink the water; we have no other choice. This is our environment.

from *Our Polluted World. Can Man Survive?* by John Perry

Check

1. Which two stretches of water does the author compare?

2. What is different about the creek now from when the early settlers found it?
What, for example, is in place of (a) the settlement (b) the cornfields (c) the trees (d) the green banks (e) the clear water?

3. Does the author think that Americans (a) are too clean (b) are not clean enough (c) delude themselves that they are clean (d) only pretend to be clean?

4. What examples are there of 'American cleanliness' in the text? Think about (a) TV advertising (b) washing up (c) bed-linen (d) bathrooms and kitchens.

5. In what sense is pollution like a struggle between the Good Guys and the Bad Guys?

6. Why would it be impossible to clean up the creek?

7. Why is the lake which the author is swimming in deceptive?

1.

Even a woodland spring cannot be trusted *unless* it has been tested = *if* it has *not* been tested.

Compare this with:

A woodland spring can be trusted . . .

provided (that) *as long as* . . .	it has

Statements with 'unless' and 'if. . .not' tend to have a negative meaning, the main message being: 'You *can't* trust even a woodland spring'. Statements with 'provided' and 'as long as' tend to have a positive meaning: 'You *can* trust a woodland spring.'

Rewrite the following sentences twice: first using unless **and then using** provided that **or** as long as, **like this:**

If we don't stop them now, it'll be too late.
(a) Unless we stop them now, it'll be too late.
(b) Provided we stop them now, it won't be too late.
or As long as . . .

We must do something positive or the whole river will be polluted.
If nobody protests, all the fish will die.
If they don't ban heavy lorries, this area will be impossible to live in.

2.

The Good Guys seek laws to *stop* / *prevent* } the Bad Guys *from poisoning* the air.

Look at these slogans:

SAY NO TO NUCLEAR POWER!
SAVE THE WHALE!
STOP THE SEAL SLAUGHTER!
BAN THE HEAVY LORRIES!
SAY NO TO INSECTICIDES!
BOYCOTT PLASTIC NOW!

Make your protests like this:

We want a law to stop/prevent them from using nuclear power.

Use these verbs in your sentences:
use kill slaughter drive spray package

3.

It's all very well protesting about nuclear power, *but* how are they going to get enough energy to run industries?

In pairs, make a short conversation about each point, like this:

– I'd like a law to prevent . . .
– It's all very well protesting about . . . but . . .

Here are some ideas to help you to counter the arguments:

the whale:	important source of food
seals:	fur industry more powerful than you think
lorries:	transport by road cheaper and more efficient than rail
insecticides:	many crops destroyed by disease without insecticides
plastic:	tougher and more hygienic than other forms of packaging.

7 Writing

Imagine that you live in a small village. The government want to build a motorway next to the village, thus enabling heavy traffic to bypass a nearby town. In pairs or groups discuss the situation and note down two arguments *for* building the motorway and two arguments *against* it.

Complete the following letter of protest to a newspaper. In the first and third paragraphs supply a suitable verb in the correct form. In the second paragraph, supply your own ideas.

Dear Sir,

I am ...... to ...... about the Government's plans to ...... a motorway through the village of X. It is all very well ...... good road communications for lorries but have you ...... the residents of X?

Important as it is to ...... and to ......, the objections seem nevertheless to be stronger. Not only ...... but also ...... What is more, ...

In my opinion it is high time the Government were prevented from ...... and also from ...... just as they please.

Yours faithfully,
B.C. Harvey
B. C. Harvey

Write a similar letter of protest about a decision to ban cyclists from important roads in the capital city.

Oral exercises

1. Listing reasons

Why wouldn't you like to live in Sri Lanka?
Well, in the first place it's too hot and secondly it's too far away.

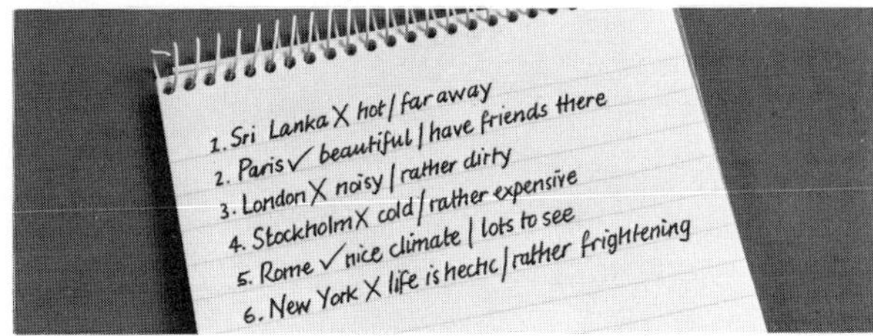

2. Countering suggestions

I think we should buy a dog.
It's all very well buying a dog, but how are we going to look after it?

1. buy dog/look after it?
2. buy car/afford to run it?
3. get a piano/get it into the house?
4. economise on heating/keep warm?
5. protest about nuclear power/run our industry?
6. cut rates and taxes/pay for essential services and quality of life?

3. Agreeing with conditions

Mark and Patti are talking about a project to supply warm clothes, food and blankets for victims of a recent earthquake. They are wondering if the project will work.

MARK: As long as we've got transport the project stands a chance of succeeding.
PATTI: *Yes, provided we've got transport, it'll work.*

1. As long as we've got transport the project stands a chance of succeeding.
2. And we want the authorities behind us.
3. Of course we must advertise.
4. Let's hope the public respond.
5. As long as they don't give us useless things.
6. And, of course, we must get it to the distribution centres quickly.

4. Talking about rules

A swimming pool attendant is talking to a new employee on the first day.

WOMAN: *First of all, you must stop them from running round the edge.*
MAN: Right. Anything else?
WOMAN: *And then, you must . . .*

Start your explanations with, 'First of all . . .' 'And then . . .' and for No. 6 'And finally . . .'

1. It is dangerous to run round the edge.
2. It is dangerous to push people in.
3. It is dangerous to jump on to people.
4. Please don't shout and scream.
5. In the interests of hygiene please do not enter the pool before having a shower.
6. Please do not wear flippers and goggles.

Unit 12 Study focus

Interaction

FUNCTION	STRUCTURE
1. Expressing opinions objectively	NP + 'is considered / 'thought / 'said } to be'
2. Linking facts in writing	Present participle 'Lying off . . ., the island is . . .' Past participle: 'Rubber, produced in . . ., is . . .'
3. Supporting preferences with reasons	'I'd prefer . . .' 'Although . . .' 'In the first place . . .' 'Secondly . . .' 'Thirdly . . .'
4. Expressing conditions	'Unless' 'Provided (that)' 'As long as' + present/pres. perfect
5. Countering arguments	'It's all very well' + verb (ing), 'but . . .'

Vocabulary

Stress in two-syllable words: nouns and verbs
Geography: types of area, landscape, climate, natural resources and disasters
Environmental pollution
Verbs: stop/prevent somebody from verb(ing)

Writing skills

1. Note-taking
2. Guided paragraphs: geographical description
3. Composition: imaginative narration and description
4. Gap-filling: letter of protest
5. Letter of protest

Unit 13 Market factors

1 Fireworks

FAWKES, Guy (1570–1606).
Yorkshire Catholic, who with other conspirators planned to blow up the Houses of Parliament in London on November 5th 1605 with gunpowder placed in the cellars. This became known as the 'Gunpowder Plot'. Fawkes undertook to watch the cellar himself, unaware that the plot had been discovered. He was arrested on November 4th, tortured and executed by hanging, after revealing the names of the other conspirators. Since then, Guy Fawkes Day has been celebrated in England with fireworks and the burning of Fawkes in effigy – 'the Guy'.

An industry in decline?
Mavis Redman examines some of the causes and effects of change in a once sparkling industry.

The survivors

Recent years have seen the gradual decline of the number of British firework manufacturers. This decline has been caused partly by the enormous investment needed to maintain large area-covering explosives factories and partly because of the cash-flow problems which come about when a year's takings are concentrated into a short three-week period in the middle of the autumn.

In Britain, only six firms are licensed to make fireworks. The biggest of these is Standard, a public company based in the north-east, in Huddersfield. Standard claims to have a 60% share of the market. Next in line is the Scottish-based firm of Brock's Fireworks, which says that it has 30% of the market. Asta claims 30% too. Down the scale we have Haley and Weller, who estimate their share at 20%. This leaves the last two, Pains Fireworks and Kimbolton Fireworks, with a very small share of the market indeed.

How the market for fireworks is divided up

It is clear from the figures that, in the firework industry, optimism is one of the qualities needed to keep going. But there are other factors as well which spell danger to a once thriving industry.

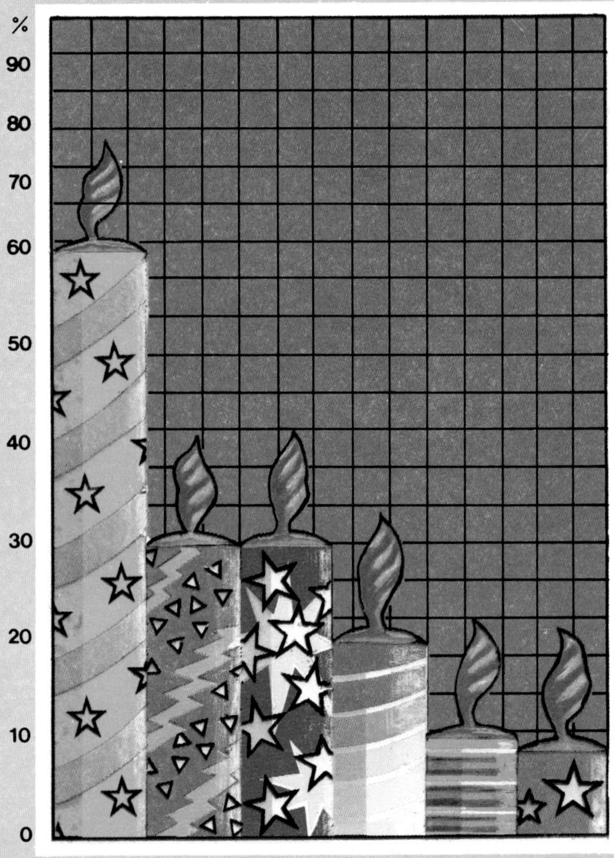

Marketing limitations

In the crucial selling period for the firework industry, that is to say, the three weeks leading up to November 5th, two factors are severely limiting their over-the-counter sales. First, it is illegal to sell fireworks in supermarkets because of the fire risk: it is all too easy for a customer to drop a lighted cigarette into a box of explosives. Secondly, only people over the age of sixteen are permitted to buy fireworks. Consequently, the increased spending power of the 10–16 age-group remains untapped by the firework industry.

Bonfire night accidents

On top of this, there is the constant barrage of propaganda from organisations such as the Campaign for Firework Reform, an organisation which has been arguing for a complete ban on selling fireworks over the counter. They argue that fireworks are a very dangerous form of amusement when handled by children or amateurs. The increasing number of accidents in recent years on November 5th, involving serious and often permanent injury to young children, shows conclusively that the sale of fireworks should be banned and that only licenced displays should be permitted.

Home Office statistics for 1979

No. treated in hospitals	745
No. of children under 13	308

Other contributing factors

There are other factors too which make the future of the firework industry bleak and difficult to forecast. The recession has meant that not so many people are prepared to indulge themselves in a celebration in which, quite literally, their money goes up in flames. The weather moreover plays its part, for there is nothing like a few rainy days at the beginning of November to discourage people from organising bonfire and firework parties in their back gardens. Finally, the growth of public firework displays, often organised by local public authorities for charity, has meant that the few remaining UK companies in the pyrotechnic business are struggling for survival.

1. Read the article on the preceding pages again and complete the following notes:

Underlying causes of the decline of the firework industry
(i) enormous investment needed to . . .
(ii) . . . .

Contributing factors
(i) illegal to sell . . . (ii) . . . (iii) . . . (iv) . . . (v) . . .

CAUSE	EFFECT
As a result of . . . / *Because of* . . . / *Owing to* . . . } . . . the bad weather *As* the weather was so bad *Since* the weather was so bad	the firework party had to be cancelled.

Look at your notes above and write different examples of the causes of the decline in the firework industry, like this:

CAUSE	EFFECT
As a result of the enormous investment needed to maintain large explosive factories *Because of* . . .	the firework industry has begun to decline.

Complete the left-hand column only. Vary the 'cause linker' each time.

2.

Only people over the age of 16 are permitted to buy fireworks. *Consequently,* / *Therefore,* } the increased spending power of the 10–16 age group remains untapped.

Expand the following notes and link the sentences below using therefore **or** consequently.

Explosive factories cover large areas/large investment needed to maintain them.
Takings restricted to limited period in year/often cash-flow problems.
Fireworks can cause serious accidents/people more concerned about home firework displays.
The Campaign for Firework Reform says misuse of fireworks cause accidents/argue complete ban on over-the-counter sales.
The country at the moment undergoing recession/fewer people prepared to spend money on fireworks.
Weather often bad early November/people discouraged from organising firework displays.

Word study

Complete the following sentences using a derivative form (i.e. base form + suffix) of the base word printed in capital letters. Mark which syllable is stressed in each word. Use a dictionary to help you if you are not sure.

ECONOMY

1. We're a bit short of money so we'd better *economise* on the fireworks this year.
2. I always use this brand of cooking oil. It's quite expensive but I find it more . . . in the long run.
3. I studied politics and . . . at college. What about you?

INDUSTRY

1. Most companies have suffered from . . . disputes over the last few years.
2. He's not particularly imaginative but he's certainly . . . .

OPTIMISM

1. I'm not too . . . about the future of the industry.
2. Only an . . . would set up a firework display on a night like this!
3. He put forward his ideas about the future of the company very . . . but I doubt if they were accepted by the majority present at the meeting.

PRODUCT

1. The company needs to launch a new . . . if it is to keep up with its competitors.
2. The . . . of a new line in fireworks was on the agenda.
3. If we are going to meet our overseas orders, we must make a . . . deal with the unions.
4. She works hard but she's not particularly . . .

3. In pairs, imagine that one of you is a young teenager of about 14, and the other is a parent. Use the guidelines below to make or write a conversation about a bonfire night party.

TEENAGER: *Suggest party with fireworks.*
PARENT: *Express worry about accidents and fire risk.*
TEENAGER: *Suggest precautions.*
PARENT: *Mention the expense.*
TEENAGER: *Suggest using own pocket money/guests bring own fireworks.*
PARENT: *Predict possible bad weather.*
TEENAGER: *Suggest that people can watch from inside the house.*
PARENT: *Express concern about pet animal.*
TEENAGER: *Suggest locking it in.*
PARENT: *Suggest alternative entertainment: local firework display – bigger and better.*
TEENAGER: *Reject suggestion: more fun at home.*
PARENT: *Concede and agree to have a few fireworks in the garden but make your conditions clear.*
TEENAGER: *Thank parent and agree to conditions.*

2

Keep fireworks sparkling!

The Golden Rain Fireworks Company

'We have been bringing out new posters but it is the traditional ones which people respond to'

Cheryl Cummings
SALES INVESTIGATOR

Main concern: increasing sales; improving advertising; creating different markets.

'I believe that the retail side is dropping because of the anti-firework lobby and cost'

Barry Underwood
MARKETING MANAGER & CHAIRMAN

Main concern: attitude of public towards domestic fireworks: safety aspect.

'The French will spend more on fireworks on Bastille Day than we spend in a whole year'

Susan Grierson
COMPANY SECRETARY

Main concern: underlying causes of decline and long-term decisions about the future of the company.

Memo

To all employees

re Open Management

In order to keep you all informed about the state of the company, there will be a general meeting in the staff canteen. We hope to outline the state of the company in what you will understand are difficult times, and to give you all a chance to make proposals for our future development and growth. The following will give reports and recommendations on their special areas:

1 Cheryl Cummings - Sales Investigator
2 Susan Grierson - Company Secretary
3 Barry Underwood - Marketing Manager and Chairman

Golden Rain Fireworks

Agenda

1 Minutes of last meeting

2 Reports on current state of affairs:

Mr Underwood: The public attitude towards domestic fireworks

Ms Cummings: Marketing problems

Ms Grierson: Underlying financial problems of GRF

3 Short and long-term proposals for the future of the company. (All suggestions welcome)

4 Any other business

1. Below is a list of all the proposals which the three representatives from the Board of Directors are going to make. Sort out who might make which proposals. Fill in the number of the proposals next to the correct name, like this:

	Proposal number
Barry Underwood	1
Cheryl Cummings	
Susan Grierson	

PROPOSALS AND IDEAS FOR THE FUTURE DEVELOPMENT OF GOLDEN RAIN FIREWORKS COMPANY

1. reduce number of dangerous fireworks such as Thunder Flashes, Jumping Crackers, Big Bangers, and Crackerjacks
2. establish contact with companies and propose use of fireworks in advertising and public relations campaigns
3. carry out research in the use of public fireworks in other countries such as Malta, France, Yugoslavia and Mexico
4. investigate possibilities of export of major firework displays for occasions such as centenary celebrations, royal occasions and national days
5. advertise in national and local newspapers
6. distribute firework code of practice to all retail outlets
7. change attitude of public to think of firework display packs and not loose fireworks to be sold in shops
8. co-operate with Campaign for Firework Reform
9. reduce explosive content of fireworks
10. diversify into military and agricultural use of fireworks
11. develop advertising campaign to encourage use of fireworks for other celebrations e.g. Christmas and New Year, Halloween, royal birthdays and public holidays

2. Roleplay

Divide into groups of three or four. You are members of the Board of Directors and have come to the meeting to discuss the future of Golden Rain Fireworks. One of you will be Barry Underwood. He will also chair the meeting. One will be Cheryl Cummings and one will be Susan Grierson. The fourth can assess the proposals of the other three and put forward any ideas he/she may have of his/her own.

First, prepare what you are going to say at the different points of the meeting. Remember that the purpose of the meeting is to come to some agreement over policy regarding the future development of the company. The fourth member of the group should take notes on any important decisions made.

Useful phrases for meetings:

COUNTERING AN ARGUMENT

It's all very well ..... but what about .....?
Yes, but have you considered .....?

INTERRUPTING

Sorry to interrupt but .....
If I may interrupt for a moment .....

FOCUSSING

As regards marketing .....

ASKING FOR AND GIVING CLARIFICATION

What exactly do you mean by .....?
/when you say ....?
By ....., I mean .....
When I say ....., I mean .....

GENERALISING

On the whole/In general .....

SUMMARISING

To sum up, ...
To conclude, ...
In conclusion, it seems that .....

3. In writing, report the proposals made and any discussion that arose from them, like this:

Mr Underwood	proposed suggested	*that they reduce* *that they should reduce* *reducing*

the number of dangerous fireworks and everyone agreed that this would be a good idea.

or

but Ms Cummings	argued said replied pointed out	that the so-called

'dangerous' fireworks were always the most popular ones.

In the end it was decided that .....

3 **LONDON–Thames TV's long-planned $12 million drama series *Clemmie*, based on the life of Lady Churchill, is the first major casualty of the big cut-back in programing ordered by Britain's ITV chiefs in the face of a projected collapse in advertising revenue for 1981.... The series, a pet project of producer Stella Richman, has been canceled by the Thames board, with program controller Nigel Ryan saying, 'In the present economic climate this production was simply too expensive'.**

... The sudden cancelation prompted Richman, who has been working on the series for 18 months, to say she will now quit TV for good. 'The time has come to call it a day,' she said... Thames is not alone in wielding the big ax on programs. Due to the recession in ad revenue, London Weekend TV has ordered a 5% cutback, and Granada TV in Manchester is also trimming its program sails... Yorkshire TV in the north tried to restrict its economies to non-program areas, but is now critically examining all production costs... Producers have been ordered to find cheaper ways of working and to cut down on foreign location filming...

A special report prepared by stockbrokers Illingworth and Henriques predicts it could be 1985 before the ad business improves. But falling revenue is not the only reason for the cuts. The launching of Britain's fourth TV channel in 1982 will cost the ITV companies around $170 million in the first year alone, so saving is the order of the day. Meanwhile the BBC continues with its own $300 million economy campaigns and the results should begin to show in leaner programs next year.

Note

American English spelling

programing, program = programming, programme
canceled = cancelled
ax = axe

Check

Which programme has been cancelled?
On whose life was it based?
How much was it to cost?
Which TV company had planned it?
What was the name of the producer?
How long has she been working on the series?
What prompted her to leave?
Which other companies are having to economise?

1. Using information from the article, find the missing cause or effect in the following chart.

CAUSE	EFFECT
(i) (a) Drop in advertising revenue (b)	General cutbacks in programmes in all companies
(ii)	Cancellation of *Clemmie*
(iii) Cancellation of *Clemmie*	....
(iv) Need to find cheaper ways of working	....

2. Make sentences like this from the information in the chart.

Because of/As a result of ....., all TV companies have been forced to make general cutbacks in programmes.

or

Advertising revenue has recently dropped. *Consequently* .....

3. Summarise the article, using this guide:

To sum up, owing to the ..... and the ....., all ITV companies ..... This has meant ..... production costs, and consequently ..... foreign location filming and ..... certain programmes. One particular example is the ....., a 12 million dollar drama series ....., as a result of which the producer ..... However, it is not only ITV which is having such problems. The BBC ..... campaign which should result in .....

4 Listening

Listen to two people talking about the effects of the recession on their business. Note down what actions they took to combat the effects of the recession.

5 Writing

Write a composition on one of the following topics:
'The effect of tourism on my country'.

or

'How have modern means of communication altered the pattern of our daily lives in the 20th century?'

Give your composition an introduction, two or more main paragraphs, and a conclusion.

Oral exercises

1. Reporting a meeting

Kevin Sykes was unable to attend the meeting of Golden Rain Fireworks staff. He had some ideas of his own, however, and he talked to Delia, who did attend.

KEVIN: Well, I think we should reduce the number of dangerous fireworks. (Underwood/suggest)
DELIA: *That's what Mr Underwood suggested.*
KEVIN: The trouble is, they are the most popular ones. (Cummings point out)
DELIA: *That's what Ms Cummings pointed out.*

1. Well, I think we should reduce the number of dangerous fireworks. (Underwood/suggest)
2. The trouble is, they are the most popular ones. (Cummings/point out)
3. I suppose we could reduce the explosive content of the fireworks instead. (Underwood/propose)
4. And it might be a good idea to advertise more in the national and local press. (Cummings/suggest)
5. On the other hand, that would annoy the anti-firework campaigners. (Underwood/say)
6. One thing we could do is look at different uses of fireworks and pyrotechnology in general. (Grierson/suggest)

2. Making suggestions

Two people at a TV company are talking about different ways of saving money.

Did anyone suggest that we cut down on secretarial staff?
Yes, I suggested cutting down on secretarial staff.

1. suggest reduce expense accounts
2. propose trim production costs
3. consider spend less on advertising
4. suggest have all telephone bills checked
5. object to save on heating
6. recommend economise on foreign travel

3. Describing cause and effect

At the same TV company

CAUSE		EFFECT
1. As a result of ...	RECESSION	make certain redundancies
2. As ...		cut certain programmes
3. Owing to ...		cut down on production costs
4. Because of ...		abolish expense accounts
5. Since ...		suspend foreign filming
6. As a result of ...		postpone wage increases

What's happening in your company?

1. *Well, as a result of the recession, we've had to make certain redundancies.*
2. *Well, as we're in the middle of a recession, we've had to cut certain programmes.*

Give alternative replies to the questions, using the notes.

4. Word study

Listen and re-express the following statements using these words:

1. economise 3. productive 5. economical
2. optimistic 4. industrious

1. Let's try and cut down on our spending this month.
   Let's try and economise this month.
2. I'm not too hopeful about next year's sales figures.
3. We need to produce more goods if we're going to make a profit.
4. I wish more people worked as hard as Mrs Standon does.
5. I find that using four-star petrol saves money in the long run.

Unit 13 Study focus

Interaction

FUNCTION	STRUCTURE
1. Expressing cause and effect	i) with phrase markers: 'as a result of' 'because of' / 'owing to' } +NP ii) with clause markers: 'as' / 'since' } +NP+VP
2. Expressing result	'Consequently,' ... 'Therefore,' ...
3. Reporting suggestions and proposals	'Ms Carr suggested ... / proposed ... that they'+past tense 'that they should'+verb +verb (ing)

ADDITIONAL STRUCTURES
Other verbs taking 'ing' form
'mind', 'consider', 'object to', 'recommend'

Vocabulary

General business: finance and marketing
Derivative forms with suffixes
Strategies for formal meetings
Verbs of reporting

Writing skills

1. Guided dialogue
2. Gap-filling: summary
3. Note-taking from listening
4. Composition: cause and effect

Unit 14 Future perfect?

Before you start:

What inventions – or gadgets invented in your lifetime – are essential to your quality of life?
What gadgets which you use in your daily life do you think you could live without?
If you had to choose three gadgets to have for the rest of your life, which would you choose?

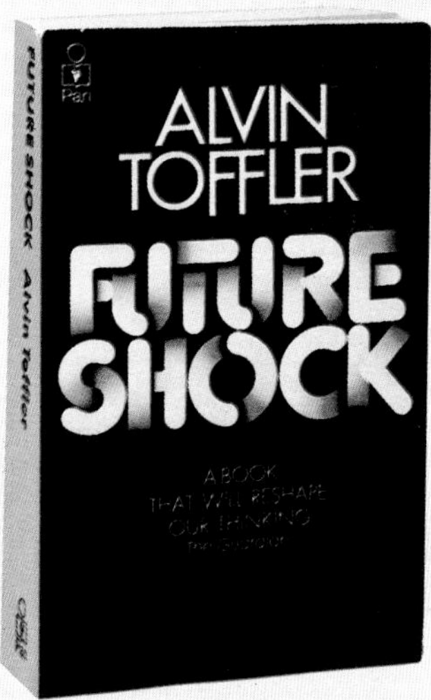

❶ Future Shock

1. Read the dialogue and then, in pairs, use the chart to make predictions about the future.

– You know the *Guardian* says that this book *Future Shock* by Alvin Toffler is 'a book to change the future'.
– Really?
– Yes, Toffler says that our lives are changing so fast that people don't know what to do. He tries to show us how to come to terms with the future.
– Huh! There won't be any future at the rate we're going! Or we'll all be living on the moon.
– No, seriously. Listen. About technical innovations it says that 'these range from new power sources, new airborne and submarine vehicles, three-dimensional photography to human hibernation for medical purposes and totally new concepts in food'.
– Interesting. Talking of food, I read somewhere that by the year 1990, it is forecast that 25% of our meat consumption will have been replaced by some sort of meat substitute.

By the year 1990, In the near future, In fifteen years' time, This time next year,	we aeroplanes a cure for cancer cars famine food as we know it most wild life petrol in cars oil tropical forests deserts ordinary TV marriage the whole world	will be may/could/will have been	using . . . living . . . eating . . . working . . . destroyed. replaced by . . . discovered.

❷ The wonderful world of gadgetry

– What on earth's that? – It's a spelling machine.	OBJECT
– What's it for? – It's a machine/a gadget/an instrument/a thing/a tool *for teaching/helping* children to read.	DEFINITION AND FUNCTION
It looks a bit like a small, compact typewriter / a large pocket calculator with letters on a keyboard. It's electronic. It can run on batteries or on electricity.	DESCRIPTION
– How does it work? – *You press* a button to start a spelling programme and a tinny voice says 'Spell "heart"' or some other word. The child then tries to spell the word *by pressing* the right letter on the keyboard. As the letters *are pressed, they appear* in the display box above the keyboard. If the child spells the word wrongly, then the voice says 'That's wrong.' If the word is correct, the voice says 'That is correct. Now spell "swan"' *so as to/in order to* take the child through a preselected spelling programme. The machine is *programmed* to spell the word correctly after five attempts. It also tells you how well you did at the end.	PROCESS

1. In pairs, use the chart below to make a similar conversation.

Object	Automatic vending machine
Purpose	To dispense hot or cold drinks
Description	Like a large cabinet or fridge/with buttons/slot for coins/run by electricity/holder for plastic or paper cups/
Process	Select/put in/press/ wait/take out if . . ., press for return . . .

2. In groups, describe to the others a gadget or a machine designed to be used in the home, in the garden, for entertainment, for use in the office or for education.

3. Writing

Write two or three paragraphs about the gadget or machine you described to your group.

❸ Future Now

The magazine that looks at the fascinating world of today's and tomorrow's advances in technology.

Contents

Look at the contents list and decide what each article might be about. Then match each of the extracts below with the right article in 'Future Now'. Tell your partner which articles you would like to read and give your reasons.

(i) Dragline excavators, as their name suggests, have a dragging rather than a shovelling action. First the bucket is raised well clear of the ground by winching in the hoist rope.

(ii) In the region immediately around the star, gravity would still be strong enough to stop light from escaping, and so a star like this would have a region of space around it where light could not escape to the rest of the universe.

(iii) Programmable mechanical workers are now being used as a matter of course in many industries throughout the world. Robots – walking, talking and particularly working robots – are not really a thing of the distant future.

(iv) And on the horizon are plans to build an underground air-pressure train system that will take people from New York to Los Angeles in less than 45-minutes at a top speed that approaches 8,000 km/h (5,000 mph). That's some indication of the transportation speed-up that future years hold for us.

(v) One of the most remarkable tools at the disposal of the modern doctor is an optical instrument which allows him to look right inside the patient's body.

(vi) At the rear of the orbiter are three large rocket engines: during launch these are fed with fuel from an external tank strapped to the orbiter's belly. This external tank falls away as the Shuttle reaches orbit, burning up in the atmosphere.

(vii) Turn a corner on the large screen. You spot a building in the distance. Tap the small screen at your left hand and you're standing right outside. It's a restaurant. Tap the screen again and you're looking at the dining room. Tap again and you're examining the menu: the world is at your fingertips with 'total television'.

❹ Teaching machines to talk

1 In the realms of science fiction, man has for years been talking to machines. No modern science fiction film is complete without its wise and articulate – if sometimes malfunctioning or downright disobedient – computer. Hal, the smooth-voiced controller of the Jupiter probe in the film *2001: A Space Odyssey,* is a perfect example of the breed.

2 But what is the reality? Are machines like these ever likely to be built?

Left *Hal, the computer from the film* 2001: A Space Odyssey, *is a classic example of a talking machine from science fiction.*

1. Copy down the *topic* or *key sentence* from the text on the left. What specific example is given?
2. What questions link the opening paragraphs to the rest of the article?
3. Do you expect the rest of the article to say, approximatley
   (a) No, they aren't?
   (b) Yes, they are?
   (c) Maybe, but not yet because there are problems?

3 There are, in the real world, two separate problems: first, getting the machine to recognize and respond to speech; and second, getting it to convert its response into speech. The second objective – making a machine that talks – is simpler than the first.

1. What are the two separate problems?
2. Which is easier to achieve?
3. Which is the author of the article likely to discuss first?

4 Modern electronic speaking machines use two basic principles. In the first, concatenated speech synthesis, a computer is used to store a 'dictionary' of spoken syllables – all possible vowel-consonant and consonant-vowel combinations – in the language concerned. To form a word, the computer draws the required syllables from its store and strings them together in the right order – 'com-pu-ter', for example. Then it adds pauses and intonation to make the output intelligible.

5 The concatenated speech method is very rigid, and produces low-quality speech. But it works quickly and is cheap to build.

6 The other method, synthesis by rule, does not store sounds or combinations of sounds, but rather a guidebook of the electronic 'rules' which are necessary to make those sounds. Synthesis by rule produces a rather better quality speech, but because many elaborate rules are needed to produce even a short string of speech sounds, the machine takes a long time to synthesize the speech.

1. These three paragraphs describe how electronic speaking machines work. What are the two basic principles?
2. Complete the following summary of these paragraphs:
   The difference between . . . and . . . is that the first draws on a . . . of spoken syllables and . . . them together, and the second draws on a . . . which can generate those sounds.
3. Describe the advantages and disadvantages of each method by completing this chart:

	FOR +	AGAINST –
Method 1		
Method 2		

4. Have you ever seen a speaking machine or heard one described? What did it do? Was it useful or efficient?

7 Using concatenated speech synthesis, several kinds of speaking machines are already commonplace, especially in the US. Talking calculators can speak each number as you punch it on the keyboard, and then read out the result. Small speaking machines, slightly bigger than a calculator, help teach children spelling. Another small machine not only plays a very good game of chess but speaks the moves as they are made.

8 A 'speaking' machine is the basis of a system used in the US by the Bell Telephone Company to improve the efficiency, and reduce the cost, of some services normally provided by human operators. A keyboard similar to a typewriter, but smaller, is plugged into a telephone set. To find a subscriber's number, you dial directory enquiries and tap out his name and address on the keyboard. The computer at the other end of the line searches its memory bank, finds the number and, using machine speech, transmits the answer to the telephone.

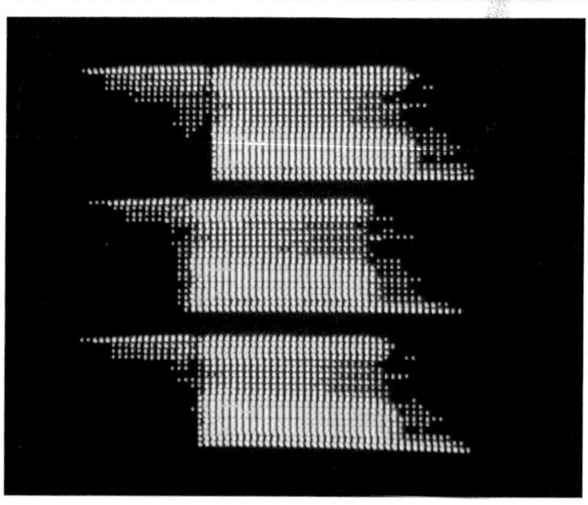

Right *A computer analyzes the sound of the word 'sum'. (1) The top two patterns represent two versions of the word by the same speaker. The bottom one is an average 'template' generated from the upper two.*

1. What examples are there of speaking machines in use in the US?
2. In the last example, explain why the operator is unnecessary.
3. Does one actually speak to the 'operator'? Why do you think this might be difficult?
4. Look back to paragraph 3. Which of these two points has the article discussed so far? What do you imagine the rest of the article to be about?

9 The next stage of development, eliminating the keyboard and allowing you simply to ask the machine for information, is a great deal harder. Any telephone directory is full of people's and companies' names, of various national origins, and many with unpredictable pronunciations. How is the machine to match your spoken request with its written – or rather, computer-coded – data? Indeed, how is this machine, or any other, going to understand your speech?

10 A vital tool for scientists trying to discover how machines might recognize speech was developed early in World War 2. This is the sound spectrograph, an electronic machine which analyzes sound waves and produces a permanent, written 'picture' of them. Just say a word, and the machine will produce an accurate, if complicated, spectrogram of the acoustic waves your voice produces. The importance of spectrogram patterns is that they can be stored (in digital form) in a computer memory. Theoretically it should be a simple matter for the computer to recognize that word again by comparing the spectrogram of any received word with the pattern in its memory.

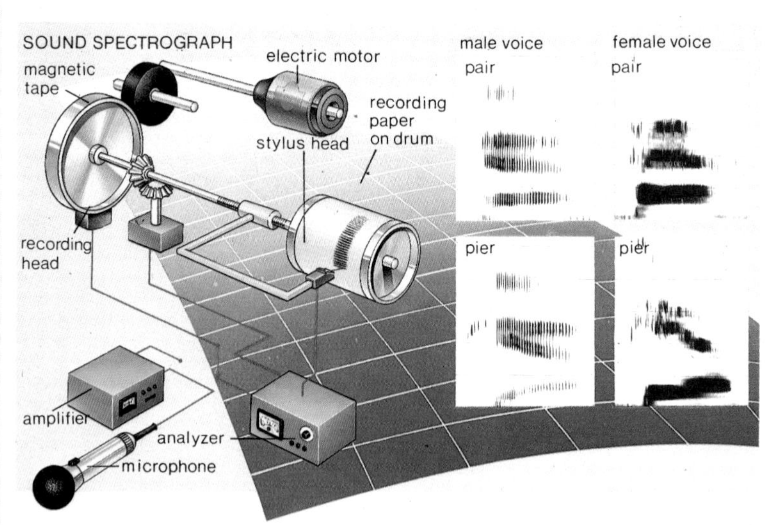

Above *The four insets are spectrograms of the words 'pair' and 'pier' spoken by male and female voices. Computers use patterns of this sort (in digital form) when comparing sounds. The similarities between the patterns are more marked when the voice is the same than when the word is the same.*

11 The catch is that no two people, even with the same regional accent, say the same word in exactly the same way. A man's voice, for example, has a much lower pitch than a woman's or a child's. His vocal tract is bigger and of a different shape. So the sounds he produces cannot possibly be the same as those produced by a woman or child. And there are quite marked differences between the sounds of individual men, individual women, individual children – that's how we 'recognize someone's voice'. There are hundreds of problems like this: identical words, spoken by different people, which produce markedly different and confusing spectrogram patterns.

1. What is an obvious difficulty connected with asking a robot for telephone directory entries?
2. The root form of 'mechanical' is 'machine'. From paragraphs 9, 10 and 11, find words which have these roots:
   develop inform nation pronounce predict
   important theory region different marked
3. Complete the following explanation of a spectrogram:
   A spectrogram is like a ... of a spoken word. In other words, you say a word and the machine will ... . In this way, a spectrograph can store ... computer memory. So when a person speaks, it should be able to compare ... with ... in its memory. The problem is that ... same way. There are very clear differences, for example, between a man and a ..., and between ... and ....

12 Even if a machine could be trained to recognize words – an example might be a drinks-dispensing machine, to which you could say 'tea', 'milk', 'sugar' – the step upwards from understanding isolated words to understanding connected speech – whole phrases and sentences – is so big that few researchers have tackled it.

13 The only reason that we understand speech is that we are familiar with our own environment, the world about us. Without that knowledge, speech would be just a jumble of noise. To understand speech, a machine too would have to understand its environment. It could do this by collecting data through electronic sensory devices, just as babies do through their eyes, ears, noses and hands. It would, in short, have to be a model human being – devoid of feelings and emotions perhaps, but in other ways just as intelligent.

1. What is the next step after understanding isolated words?
2. Why is this the most difficult part?
3. How would the computer compare with a human being if this were possible?

Summarise the whole article by making a plan with headings and notes containing the most important points the author makes.

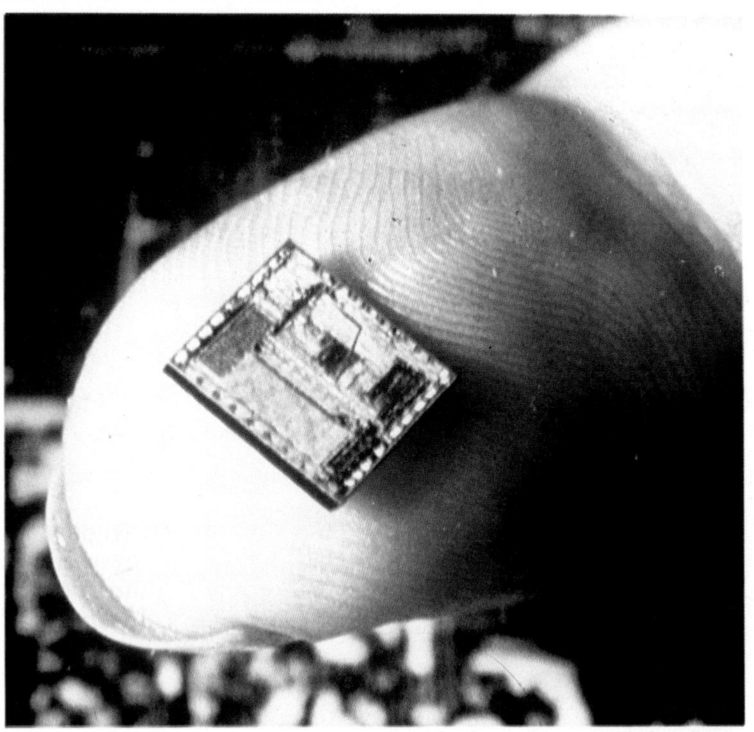

Above *The silicon chip is an essential element of any speech-recognition machine. Only computers have the power to analyze and compare human speech patterns.*

5 . . . something which would improve the world we live in

1. Discussion

In pairs or groups, choose two or three subjects which interest you from the list below.

Agriculture and food production
Lifestyle – the home/entertainment/leisure
Communications technology
Conservation
Crime prevention
Education
Energy and natural resources
Environment
Industry and commerce
Science and medicine
Space exploration
Travel and transportation
Weather control
Undersea exploration

Suggest, with reasons, one or two innovations or inventions you would like to see. Where appropriate, suggest an area of the world where you think your idea would have some benefit. State its function or purpose and make any conditions your idea would have to fulfil.

Finally, in your group, choose the three ideas that you all think would be most beneficial to the world.

2. Writing

'An idea which I think could help the world.'

(i) Look at these notes a student in Nairobi made for her essay:

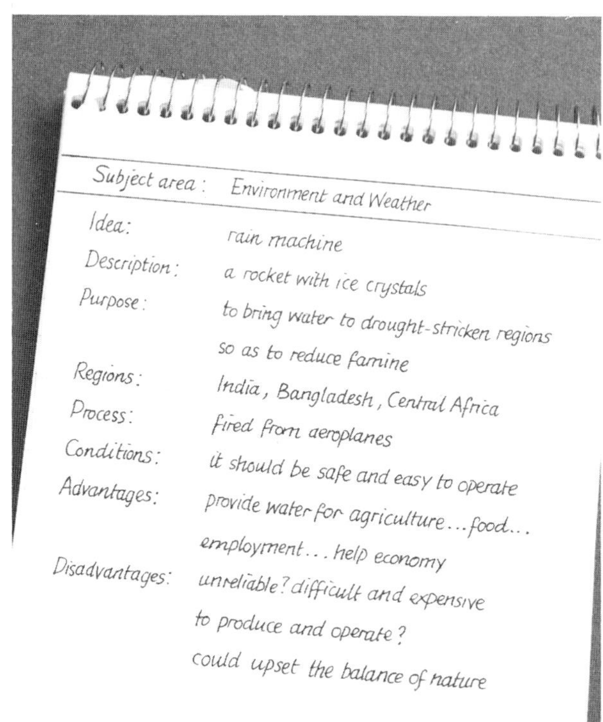

Subject area: Environment and Weather

Idea: rain machine
Description: a rocket with ice crystals
Purpose: to bring water to drought-stricken regions so as to reduce famine
Regions: India, Bangladesh, Central Africa
Process: fired from aeroplanes
Conditions: it should be safe and easy to operate
Advantages: provide water for agriculture ... food ... employment ... help economy
Disadvantages: unreliable? difficult and expensive to produce and operate? could upset the balance of nature

(ii) Choose your subject, make similar notes and then write an essay.

In paragraph 1, your *introduction*, you should outline the problem; in the *main body of the essay* you should say something about any progress that has been made towards solving the problem. Use the headings from the student's notes to give focus to your paragraphs. In your *conclusion*, your last paragraph, try to outline some of the advantages and disadvantages of your idea.

6 Listening

Listen to a college lecturer talking about computers in education. Note:
(i) the different sorts of computers he mentions (ii) what a computer can do for his students (iii) what a computer can't do.

Oral exercises

1. Making forecasts (1)

They'll never find a cure for cancer. (1990)
Oh, I think by 1990 they will have.

They'll never put a man on Mars. (50 years)
Oh, I think in 50 years' time they will have.

1. They'll never find a cure for cancer. (1990)
2. They'll never put a man on Mars. (50 years)
3. I'm sure pills will never replace food. (the 21st century)
4. I don't believe they'll ever solve the problem of world food shortage. (20 years)
5. I am convinced they'll never find a cure for diabetes. (The year 2000)
6. I don't think they would ever dare to ban the sale of cigarettes. (20 or 30 years)

2. Making forecasts (2)

Look back at Exercise 1 and make complete predictions.

1. *They say that by 1990 they will have found a cure for cancer.*

3. Describing function

Paula and Tom are in the kitchen preparing a meal.

TOM: Wait a moment, I've got an egg-slicer.
PAULA: *How useful! A gadget for slicing eggs!*

1. Wait a moment! I've got an egg-slicer.
2. Hang on! I've got a garlic-crusher for that.
3. Wait a moment! You can use my cherry-stoner if you like.
4. Just a minute! There's an apple-corer somewhere.
5. Why don't you use the juice-extractor?
6. Would you like to use my parsley-chopper?

4. Expressing purpose

Sid, the leader of a gang of bank robbers, is explaining to Mick, a new member, the purpose of all the preparations.

MICK: Why do we need masks?
SID: *So as not to be identified, you idiot!*

1. masks – identify
2. soft-soled shoes – hear
3. a get-away car – catch
4. to do it at night – see
5. to leave the country – find.

Now re-express the sentences in written form using 'in order not to'.
1. *They wore masks in order not to be identified.*

Unit 14 Study focus

Interaction

FUNCTION	STRUCTURE
1. Predicting the future	'By the year 2000, we will be using . . .' 'cars will have been replaced by . . .'
2. Describing how things work	'It's a machine for teaching children to spell'
3. Describing process	'You press a button' 'The letters are pressed'
4. Expressing purpose	'. . .so as to/in order to take the child . . . .'

ADDITIONAL STRUCTURES	
1. Time phrases with future reference	'By . . ./In . . ./This time next year'
2. Modals to express possibility	'Cars may/might have been replaced by . . .'

Vocabulary

A selection of words to do with:
electronics, machine technology, astronomy and space, computer science, language acquisition and pronunciation

Writing skills

1. Sentence writing
2. Paragraph writing: describing a gadget or machine and how it works
3. Note-taking from a text
4. Summary of text
5. Composition about inventions to help the world
6. Note-taking from listening passage.

Unit 15 Consolidation

1 Camel Lady

Before you start:
What do you know about Australia and its geography?
What do you know about the Australian Aborigines?

> Quote about *Tracks:*
>
> 'It is, however, the work of an impassioned feminist and anti-racist, and as such *Tracks* makes a joyful change from the usual dry, authoritative book-of-a-journey. Davidson may not be a writer born, but hers is a remarkable account of action, confrontation and soul-searching which I, for one, found hard to put down.'
> (Helen MacKintosh)

Charles Harvey talks to Robyn Davidson about her book *Tracks* which tells of her trek of 2,700 km (1,700 miles) through the desert of Australia with only four camels and a dog for company.

It is fairly understandable why Robyn Davidson became a celebrity almost overnight and the darling of the more sophisticated Sunday newspapers. It is also easy to see why she got labelled as the 'Camel Lady'. For there she was, young and alone, with only a few camels and a dog, trekking west, beyond civilisation, across the vast expanses of the Australian desert. Not only is she an adventuring heroine in the great tradition of explorers like Mary Kingsley, but she is a passionate feminist and anti-racist.

Tracks is her account of the three years she spent preparing for and making her incredible journey. Personal, rambling and full of the minute details of her daily life though it is, it is her admiration and concern for the Aboriginal people in Central Australia which shines out so clearly. I asked her if her determination to learn about the Aborigines had motivated her to make the trip. 'Yes, I admire Aboriginal people and their culture. Many people think that the Aborigines are a primitive and inferior people. But theirs is a sane and civilised society. Compared with them, we are power-crazed, neurotic and greedy. For example, Aborigines have lived in the desert for 40,000 years without destroying their land, without overpopulating it and without waging wars against one another. Not only that, but they've managed to survive without needing a central system of government, leaders or power groups. What's more, they cannot be accused of accumulating produce in excess of their needs like we have, nor of making

the concept of work into a sort of religion as we have done. They are a people who place great value on time – time which they use to lead a wise and extremely religious life.'

Robyn plans to use the information gained from the trek and all her considerable personal resources – financial as well as intellectual as her book has been such a success – to publicise the genocidal threat which hangs over the Aborigines and to try to raise support to prevent the genocide from happening. 'We must do something now,' she says with passion, 'in order to stop their civilisation from being wiped out.'

Of course, Robyn hates being a celebrity but she is prepared to suffer from it so as to promote her cause. Will her fame affect her future plans? 'Not in the least,' she replies. 'Although I'm going to make my next trip a private one.'

Would she write about it?

'I might,' she replied.

As regards her future plans, what are they? 'I'm going to India to stay with a friend in Rajasthan. She'll teach me Hindustani and I'll encourage her to write about her own life: she has been living in purdah for thirty years. After that, I hope to set out with the Raicas, a nomadic people who live around that area. They travel in the desert for six months a year with their goat and camel herds, and live on nothing but camel milk and cereals.'

On the whole, I feel we have not heard the last of the 'Camel Lady'.

1. Complete the reporter's notes on Robyn Davidson's trek:

Place of trek:
Length of time:
Distance travelled:
Accompanied by:
Mode of transport:
Purpose of expedition:
Immediate plans:
Future plans:
Character of Robyn Davidson:

2. Make a list of questions which the writer, Charles Harvey, would have asked to get his information for the whole article. Re-enact the interview in pairs afterwards.

3. Complete the following information:

Robyn's views on the Aborigines

Compared with us,
their society is (1) . . . (2) . . .
they are not (1) . . . (2) . . . (3) . . .
they have never (1) . . . (2) . . . (3) . . .

4. Rewrite and complete the following sentences:

(i) Many people think that the Aborigines are a primitive and inferior people.

The Aborigines . . . .

(ii) Theirs is a sane and civilised society.

Not only . . . .
As well as . . . .

(iii) Aborigines have lived in the desert for 40,000 years without destroying their land, without over-populating it and without waging war with one another.

Although . . ., they have neither . . ., nor . . .
The Aborigines cannot be accused of . . .

(iv) Robyn plans to use the information gained from the trek and all her personal resources to publicise the genocidal threat.

Using . . . .

(v) We must do something now in order to stop their civilisation from being wiped out.

Unless . . . .
As long as . . . .
She feared that unless . . . .

(vi) After learning Hindustani, I hope to set out with the Raicas.

Once . . . .

❷ Dangerous habit

1. Form groups of four or five. Find out who smokes and discuss the following questions with them:

How many cigarettes do you smoke a day?
When do you smoke? Why?
Have you ever tried to give up?
What do you imagine would be the best method?
Do you think governments ought to dissuade people from smoking, at least in all public areas?

2. In the columns opposite are parts of a complete text, arranged in the wrong order. The original text is taken from *Intimate Behaviour* by Desmond Morris.

Read the ten extracts, either individually or in groups. Work out what the words or phrases in italic refer to. Sometimes they will refer to something mentioned in another extract. Try to link the paragraphs first in this way.

Decide in which order the extracts should be and number them in the boxes provided.

3. Discussion

'It's my life and I can do what I like with it!'
With reference to smoking and other dangerous habits, how far is this a justifiable point of view?

☐ The great error of the anti-smoking campaigners is that they rarely stop and ask the basic question: why do people want to smoke in the first place? *They* seem to think it has something to do with drug addiction – with the habit-forming effects of nicotine. There is an element of *this* certainly, but it is by no means the most important factor operating. Many people do not even inhale their smoke and can be absorbing only minute amounts of the drug, so that the causes of their addiction to cigarettes must be sought elsewhere.

☐ On a hoarding in Zurich, Switzerland, there is a large poster showing a man's head reproduced twice, *one* beside *the other.* The heads are identical except for one detail: between the lips of one there is a cigarette; between the lips of the other there is instead a baby's dummy, or pacifier. It is assumed that the message is obvious, since not a single word accompanies the picture.

☐ Simply to tell people they must not do something because it is harmful may be a wise step to take, but it is also a short-term *one.* It is like using war to solve the population problem. War kills millions, but as soon as it is over there is a post-war birth bulge and the population growth goes soaring on again.

☐ *The answer* clearly lies in the act of oral intimacy involved in holding the object between the lips, as the Zurich poster so beautifully demonstrates, and *this answer* almost certainly applies as the basic explanation for the full inhalers as well. Until *this aspect of smoking* is properly investigated, there will be little long-term hope of eliminating it from our stressed, comfort-seeking cultures.

☐ A large-scale campaign to alert smokers to the dangers of filling the lungs with carcinogenic smoke has been undertaken in many countries. Cigarette promotions have been banned on television in several major areas, and there has been endless discussion of how to discourage children from taking up *the habit.* Gruesome films are shown of pathetic hospital patients in the advanced stages of lung cancer. Some smokers have responded intelligently and given up, but many others have become so alarmed that instead they have been forced to light up an extra cigarette to calm their shattered nerves. In other words, although the problem is at last being dealt with, it is by no means solved.

☐ The poster is, of course, supposed to put adult smokers to shame by making *them* feel immature and babyish, but it can also be read backwards. If the man with the dummy in his mouth is gaining some comfort from it, just like a baby, then all that is wrong with *that part of the picture* is that it looks so infantile. Now switch to *the other head* – here the problem is solved. Like the dummy, the cigarette gives comfort too, and in one stroke the babyish element is gone.

☐ *Similarly,* every time there is an anti-smoking scare, thousands of people stop smoking, but after the scare is over, the shares of the cigarette companies start to soar again.

☐ Even if we do not perversely twist the well-intended message in *this way,* it nevertheless provides us with a valuable clue concerning the world-wide smoking problem that faces society today. It is a problem that has been dealt with recently for the first time.

☐ Without realizing it, the designers of this poster have said far more about the importance of smoking than they intended. In *one simple visual statement* they have explained why so many thousands of people are prepared to risk a painful death, coughing and spewing as *their* lungs clog with cancerous cells.

☐ Seen *this way,* it might almost be an advertisement to encourage smoking in those who have not yet discovered the basic comfort of *this activity.* Smoke a cigarette and you can be pacified without feeling immature!

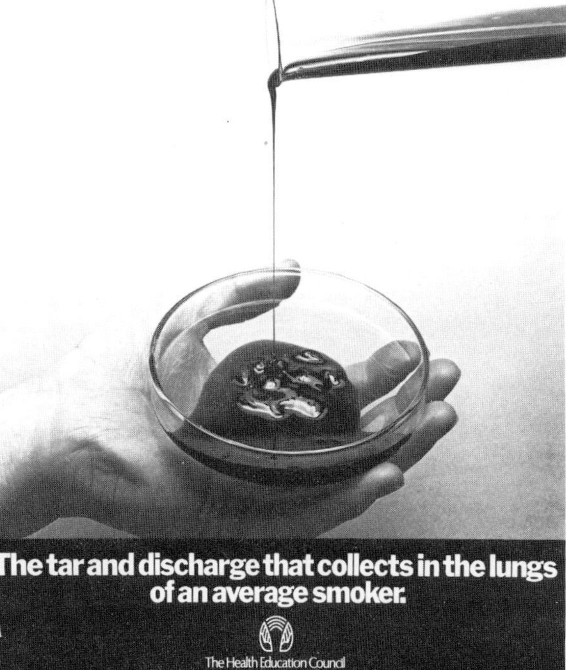

❸ Marston Hall

A study centre unique in Europe

The new College of English Studies at Cookham aims to provide a comprehensive range of courses for students of English as a Foreign Language. These range from beginners' courses through English for Special Purposes to preparatory courses for students about to attend a British university.

Apart from being one of the biggest residential centres in Europe devoted entirely to the teaching of English as a Foreign Language, the College is now superbly equipped for this task with the most sophisticated teaching aids and first-class accommodation. Details of our courses are given in the College Prospectus.

Study facilities

Marston Hall has a total of 30 study rooms accommodating 12 students in each, and three large lecture rooms, all double-glazed and air-conditioned. Each lecture room is equipped with film and slide projectors and screen, a closed-circuit TV, a tape-recorder wired to central speakers and an overhead projector. Apart from the standard equipment, each study room too is equipped with a closed-circuit TV, tape-recorder and overhead projector. Four 12-booth Tandberg language laboratories and a well-stocked tape library are also available for student practice.

The College is also fortunate to have its own TV studio with fully-trained technicians on hand to operate the cameras if students wish to put together their own programmes.

The audio-visual room, with a wide range of equipment, can be used by lecturers and students alike. A College bookshop stocks all the required course books, a selection of modern paperbacks and stationery.

On the social side, there's an attractive bar and coffee lounge. Students can meet each other in the Mayflower Bar, which has balconied alcoves and French windows leading out on to the central lawn and rose garden. For those who like a little exercise, there's an indoor heated swimming pool, clock golf and tennis courts. With enough notice we can organise trips on the Thames, to West End theatres and Stratford-on-Avon. Other recreational facilities are being planned.

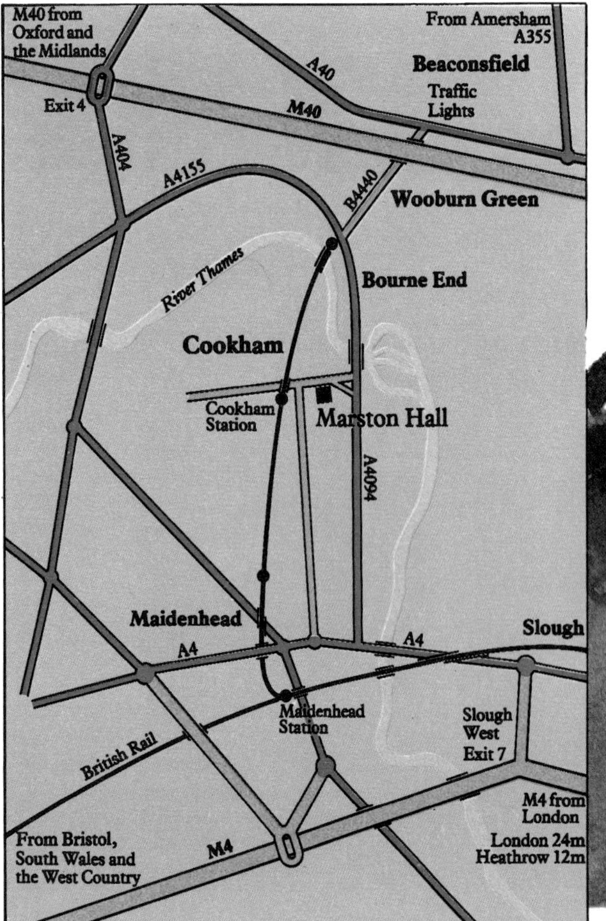

Courses at Marston Hall

General English
Level 1 Beginners
2 Pre-intermediate
3 Intermediate
4 Post-intermediate

Examination courses
5 First Certificate
6 Proficiency

Special skills courses
Pronunciation and speechwork
Letter writing
English literature
Essay writing
Conversation (advanced)
Seminar skills
Fast and efficient reading
Pre-university language skills

English for Specific Purposes
English for Secretaries
Executives
Engineers
Nurses
Doctors

College of English Studies,
Marston Hall, Cookham,
Maidenhead, Berkshire
Telephone: 94124

Check

Is Marston Hall suitable for:
- someone who is going to study at a university in Britain?
- someone who has never learnt any English before?
- lectures to large audiences?
- someone who wants to get away from the city?
- someone who simply wants to practise everyday spoken English?
- watching full-length feature films?
- someone who wants to watch him/herself speaking English in different situations?
- someone who does not want to travel anywhere for a social evening?
- someone who likes to have some exercise while studying?
- working in hot weather?

Writing tasks

1. A formal letter

Write a letter asking for further information about a particular course at Marston Hall.

2. A curriculum vitae

Choose and apply for a course at Marston Hall. Attach a curriculum vitae giving details of your educational background.

In your letter you should indicate the purpose of your study and the reasons you have for choosing Marston Hall, and your extra-curricular interests.

3. An informal letter

Imagine you are a student at Marston Hall. Write to a friend describing the college and its environment, your study programme, your leisure time and some of your friends.

4. A set of directions

Write two sets of directions: one for a person visiting you from Oxford, the other for someone coming from Heathrow Airport.

5. A notice

You are Secretary of the Social Club at Marston Hall. Write a notice persuading people to use the snack bar more often, as opposed to going out to local restaurants.

❹ Strategies magazine

This is your chance to prepare, write and produce your own class magazine. Write about the topics that interest you. Use photographs, cuttings and drawings to illustrate your magazine. The contents list below is a guide to what you could write about.

MAIN FEATURES

1. **Then all the children sing ...**
   a description of a very special festival in Bavaria.
2. **The image on the wall ...**
   the future of television in the home
3. **Lost property ...**
   a photographer explains how he lost his expensive equipment and gives some advice on how to look after your valuables
4. **Profits on the piste ...**
   the big business behind the skiing industry in Austria
5. **Treasures from the deep**
   an account of an underwater exploration beneath the Red Sea
6. **Wonderful world?**
   does the rest of the world realise the problems of living on 'the crack of the earth' in North Africa?
7. **No, thank you, nurse!**
   a nurse reveals the funny sides of working in a hospital
8. **Personality Profile: Hilda Gomez da Costa**
   some surprising facts about the well-known 'boss' of the Institute of English as a Foreign Language

REGULAR FEATURES

FICTION

9. **Devil dogs of darkness ...**
   a short story for after midnight by award-winning novelist Annie Serafim. Don't read it alone!

OUT AND ABOUT

10. **This month at the movies**
    this month's films reviewed

TRAVEL

11. **Faraway Places**
    we talk to a woman who spent last summer in Yucatan in Mexico

COOKERY CORNER

12. **Picnic time is here again!**
    easy-to-prepare salads and cold dishes for eating outdoors

HEALTH AND BEAUTY

13. **Dr Margolin suggests**
    your letters on health problems answered

To which unit in *Studying Strategies* does each article refer? Review the writing work you did in those units before you start.

Writing

In pairs or groups, prepare the articles for your magazine. You may write any of the articles suggested in the contents list *or* a similar article, e.g. you may want to write about a holiday in a different country, give recipes for different kinds of food or report on a different type of industry.

PROCEDURE

1. Plan the contents for the magazine.
2. Decide who is going to be responsible for each article.
3. Choose an editor and some assistant editors who will collect and check all the finished articles.
4. Choose an art editor who will design the magazine. Choose pictures if necessary, and put all the articles together.
5. Plan and write the articles. Remember that if you are writing a main feature article, you will need:
   - an introduction
   - two or more paragraphs for the main 'body' of the article
   - a conclusion
   - some sort of visual support (optional).
6. If you can, type your article when you are sure you cannot improve it any more.

Vote for the article you like best and give the person who wrote it the 'STRATEGIES JOURNALIST OF THE YEAR AWARD!'

Functional index

Grammatical summary

Index of writing tasks

Longman Group Limited
Longman House
Burnt Mill
Harlow
Essex
England

First published 1982
Third impression 1982
ISBN 0 582 51681 1

Among the many people who have helped to produce this book, we would especially like to thank Leila Keane for her invaluable comments on the manuscript.

Acknowledgements

We are grateful to the following for permission to reproduce copyright materiai:

Jonathan Cape Ltd. and Random House Inc. for an extract from *Intimate Behaviour* by Desmond Morris; Encyclopaedia Britannica Inc. for an adapted extract from 'Polo, Marco' in *Encyclopaedia Britannica* 14th Edition (1967); the author's agents, Dr. Herbert Fensterheim and Jean Baer for adapted extracts from *Don't Say Yes, When You Want To Say No*; The Hollywood Reporter for an adapted extract from the article 'England' 12th November 1980; Macmillan, London and Basingstoke for extracts (one adapted) and table from *The Burglary Business and You* by Peter Burden; Marshall Cavendish Ltd. for extracts from *Insight* © 1980; Margot Mellersh for an extract from 'Mackenzie' in *The Explorers* by the late H. E. L. Mellersh published by A. Wheaton & Company Ltd. 1969; Oxford University Press for an adapted extract from 'Kingsley, Mary H' *Dictionary of National Biography*; the Royal Shakespeare Company for an extract from the 1980 Stratford-upon-Avon programme for *Romeo and Juliet* © Royal Shakespeare Theatre 1980; the literary agents and Simon & Schuster Inc. for the 'Recipe for Christmas Pudding' from *Mrs. Bridges Upstairs and Downstairs Cookery Book* edited by Adrian Bailey © 1975 by Sagitta Productions Ltd. Used by permission of Deborah Rogers Ltd., London; the author's agents for the Estate of W. Somerset Maugham, William Heinemann and Doubleday & Co. for extracts from 'A Man from Glasgow' and 'A Man with a Conscience' by W. Somerset Maugham in *65 Short Stories* 1976; Syndication International Ltd. for an adapted extract from the 'Sting' interview from *Woman's Own* by Lulu Appleton 27th September 1980; *Time Out Magazine* for abridged extracts from 'Interview with Robyn Davidson' by H. O. Nazareth and 'Book Reviews' by Helen Mackintosh, 17th October 1980; The Trustees for the copyright for the late Dylan Thomas for an abridged extract from *A Prospect of the Sea* by Dylan Thomas published by J. M. Dent 1955; Franklin Watts Ltd. for an adapted extract from *Our Polluted World, Can Man Survive?* by John Perry, 1972.
We are unable to trace the copyright owners of 'Open Letter to a Trio of Thieves' published in the *Evening Standard* 16th June 1980 and an extract from a film review entitled 'The Elephant Man' and would appreciate any information which would enable us to do so.

We are grateful to the following for permission to record copyright material:

The Decca Record Company Ltd. for an extract from 'The Holly and the Ivy' from *The World of Christmas* sung by the Choir of King's College, Cambridge © 1970; Marshall Cavendish Ltd. for an extract from *How to Read Your Dreams* © 1975; The Trustees for the copyright for the late Dylan Thomas for an abridged extract from *A Prospect of the Sea* by Dylan Thomas published by J. M. Dent, 1955.
We are unable to trace the copyright owner of an adapted dialogue from *Living Decisions in Family and Community* 1974 published by the B.B.C. and would appreciate any information which would enable us to do so.

We are grateful to the following for permission to reproduce copyright photographs/illustrative material:

Bryan and Cherry Alexander for page 84; Associated Press Ltd., for page 87 (right); Aerofilms Ltd., for page 98 (middle left); A & M Records Ltd., for page 27 (bottom); Barnaby's Picture Library for pages 6 (bottom left), 56 (middle top), 80, 88, 94, 103; Biofotos for page 98 (top left); Bodleian Library for page 58; British Nursing Association for page 65 (left); British Tourist Authority for page 74 (top); BBC Hulton Picture Library for page 102; Brocks Fireworks Ltd., for page 105 (inset); Bucyrus Erie Company for page 112; Central Office of Information page 64; Cooper-Bridgeman Library for page 46; John Cleare/Mountain Camera for page 57; Carl Zeiss West Germany for page 68; Colorific Photo Library Ltd., for pages 86–87, 97, 118–119; J. Allan Cash Ltd., for page 95 (left); Douglas Dickins for page 56 (bottom middle & bottom); Elisabeth Whiting Associates for page 18; Food and Agricultural Organisation for page 116; Peter Fraenkel for pages 56 (top), 60; Ford Motor Company Ltd., for page 62 (top); George Philip & Son Ltd., London for pages 30–31; Health Education Council for page 121 (right); Intel Corporation (UK) Ltd., for page 115; John Topham Picture Library for page 10 (left); Keystone Press Agency Ltd., for page 39; Kobal Collection for page 113; Longman Photo Unit for pages 4, 15, 34, 44, 48, 120; The Mansell Collection for page 54; Mary Evans Picture Library for page 121 (left), and Mary Evan/Sigmund Freud Copyright for page 89; 'From *Insight* © Marshall Cavendish Ltd.,' for page 114 (top & bottom); New Scotland Yard for page 17; Nottingham University for page 28 (top); The National Gallery for page 47 (top right); 'Future Shock by Alvin Toffler, published by Pan Books Ltd.,' for page 110 (left); Pictor International Ltd., for pages 6–7, 11 (left); Picturepoint Ltd., for pages 6 (bottom right), 98–99, 106 (left & right); Pace Photographs for page 65 (right); The Press Association for page 71; Public Archives of Canada for page 84 (inset); Rex Features Ltd., for pages 26 & 27; Radio Times/Ric Gemmell for page 28 (bottom); Royal Geographical Society for pages 82–83; 'Programme designed by Jim Allen on behalf of the Royal Shakespeare Company' for page 78 (top); Spectrum Colour Library for pages 10 (right), 62 (bottom), 74 (bottom), 95 (right), 98 (middle right); © Seated Woman by Pablo Picasso: '© S.P.A.D.E.M. Paris, 1981'/Art Gallery of Ontario for page 47 (left); Phil Green/Sunday Times for page 67; Shostal Associates for pages 70, 98 (top right); The Tate Gallery for page 42; Texas Instruments for page 111 (right); Universal City Studios for page 51; United Artists Corporation for page 79; © 'Wadsworth Atheneum, Hartford, Connecticut.' The Ella Gallup Sumner & Mary Catlin Sumner Collection for page 47 (bottom right); Anastasi White for page 50; Reg Wilson for page 78 (bottom); Anthony Weir/Janet & Colin Bord for pages 90–91; Photo by John Warmsley from 'Waiting for the dark' by Leigh Berg & John Warmsley, Macmillan Education for page 105; 'Thrall of Hypno' by Angus McKie/Young Artists for page 110 (right); Zefa Picture Library (UK) Ltd., for pages 6 (top left), 7 (bottom), 11 (inset), 66, 106 (middle).
We have been unable to trace the copyright holders of the photographs on pages 6 (top right) and 25, and would be grateful for any information that would enable us to do so.

Designed by Nucleus Design Associates

Illustrations by: TAS for pages 10, 55, 59, 82 & 122; Tony Morris for pages 14, 15, 30, 31, 32, 33, 35, 122 & 123; Stephen Pitcher for pages 16, 64, 65 & 102; Ann Rees for pages 19 & 24; Gary Underhill for pages 22, 23, 106 & 111; Per Dahlberg for pages 28, 38, 72 & 73; Charles Front for pages 43 & 75; Ian Craig for pages 46, 47, 50, 51 & 92; Illustra for pages 63 & 80; Tony Baskeyfield for pages 81, 90 & 91.

Reproduced, printed and bound in Great Britain by
Hazell Watson & Viney Ltd, Aylesbury, Bucks